GOLF
The Mind Game

GOLF

The Mind Game

Marlin M. Mackenzie, Ed.D.
with Ken Denlinger

A DELL TRADE PAPERBACK

A DELL TRADE PAPERBACK
Published by
Dell Publishing
a division of
Random House, Inc.
1540 Broadway
New York, New York 10036

Designed by Richard Oriolo

ISBN: 0-440-50209-8
Printed in the United States of America
Published simultaneously in Canada

March 1990

20 19 18 17 16 15 14

BVG

To my brother,
Ken, for auld lang syne.

CONTENTS

ACKNOWLEDGMENTS

Lots of people shared directly and indirectly in the development of this book—athletes from many sports, my students, my agent, my collaborating author, my editor, and most of all my wife, Edna.

Several dozen outstanding golfers were exceedingly helpful because they allowed me to rummage around in their brains to find out how their minds work. And they provided the true test of the validity of my techniques when they actually performed better after using them.

My graduate students at Teachers College, Columbia University, contributed as they constantly challenged me to clearly describe and justify what I did with my clients. Their analytical minds and healthy skepticism enabled me to refine and expand my techniques.

My collaborator, Ken Denlinger, a good golfer in his own right, was a constant source of humor, understanding, encouragement, practicality, and skepticism.

My agent, Faith Hornby Hamlin, had the insight and confidence to recognize that my earliest draft of a book for athletes in general contained the seeds of a publishable book; and she obviously convinced others to agree with her.

My editor, Jody Rein, with the force of her logical analysis and organization, and with her interest in the uniqueness of my approach, guided my collaborator and me in transforming our original manuscript into a better organized and more succinct piece of work.

Edna, my wife and companion on and off the golf course,

deserves a hearty hug and unmeasurable thanks for her emotional support and for her hours of careful editing of draft after draft after draft of this book. She demanded clarity, logic, and good grammar without imposing upon me her own ideas about competition and play, about hitting a golf ball, or about mental processes.

To all of these people I say "Thanks." To the golfers among them, I say "Have a good time, and hit 'em long and straight."

MMM
Washingtonville, New York
July 1989

INTRODUCTION

People pay dearly to play golf. They wear the most expensive shoes in their closet, and they kill grass with implements that can run over a thousand dollars a set. Some pay a small fortune to determine where to play golf—and with whom. At those prices the civilized sport becomes an investment. Yet nearly all golfers, from humble hackers to elite touring pros, in dogged pursuit of enjoyment—and par—rarely invest as much as a thought on what will help them more than any hunk of high-tech equipment:

Their own minds.

I propose to change that. In this book I explain the ways your mind, more marvelous than any computer, can be tapped to improve your golf. Wouldn't you prefer feeling the ball jump from the sweet spot on your club, flying long, high, and straight rather than short, skidding dubs? Wouldn't you prefer more matches won and fewer payoffs at the 19th hole? Sure you would.

What I offer is a practical, down-to-earth system that uses the mind and emotions to regulate skills in golf—and it *works,* whether you're a weekend enthusiast or a world-class professional, a 30-handicapper playing from the white tees or a scratch player. The system works because it quiets the conscious mind and engages your unconscious resources. An active conscious mind acts like the hazards on the golf course—trapping, drowning, or blocking balls from their flight to the cup because you're *thinking* too much about your swing while playing. My techniques get you to do all your thinking about your swing on the practice tee so that your mind stays out of your way as you swing on the course.

Although golf is a complex mind game, it's also supposed to be fun. So are the exercises in this book. In Part 1 I describe the fundamentals of the mind game—how your mind operates, how to deepen awareness of your mental processes, and how to improve your game by capitalizing on your inner resources.

Part 2 contains descriptions of specific techniques, about thirty in all, that can be applied to your method of thinking and the unique way you respond emotionally to competition. These techniques are designed to help you achieve better concentration, heightened motivation, consistency of performance, increased self-confidence, recovery of lost skills, and more enjoyment. A few of them focus on the mobilization of energy when tired, faster healing after injury, and pain control.

I've coined a word that describes my perspective of how the mind works—*Metaskills*. It refers to the interaction between emotions and thoughts that regulate skillful athletic performance, most of which are out of conscious awareness. After years of coaching and thinking about the unity of mind and body, I became dissatisfied with the methods of coaching that stressed conscious thought. The methods are okay up to a point, but they don't fully represent what superb athletes really do in their minds to control their behavior.

To eliminate my dissatisfaction I studied psychology and counseling in a search for knowledge that I knew existed although I did not know exactly where to look. Finally, I decided to go to the source. I asked athletes directly how they used their minds and emotions to develop and control their skills. My training as a master practitioner in Neuro-Linguistic Programming (NLP) provided me with the knowledge to ask the right questions and the refined skills to uncover their conscious and unconscious processes.

I then created counseling techniques out of what the athletes told me. I combined their information with what I'd learned from psychology and from my coaching experience. To refine my metaskills techniques I worked directly with eighty elite athletes (male and female, ages eight to thirty-five) in eleven sports over a two-year period. The model that evolved has been working successfully for about seven years with all kinds of athletes. This book contains those techniques that are most appropriate for golfers.

The psychological perspective that I emphasize is one of understanding *how* golfers, at every level, regulate their performance, not *why* they don't play well. Believe it or not, you already possess all the necessary internal resources for playing better golf. The trick is to uncover them and put them to work. Trying to figure out the reasons why you don't hit the ball well is counterproductive. This kind of thinking taps and reinforces negative stuff in your mind, the stuff that makes you continue to swing badly and feel worse.

The mind games in this book were designed to swing your golfing mind from conscious control to automatic pilot. The ultimate goal is to have your unconscious mind in complete control during competition, except for conscious planning of each shot before addressing the ball. Seldom will there be a need for conscious application of any metaskills techniques while playing a match. If you've learned them well, they'll "kick in" automatically, just as your golf swing automatically follows a grooved pattern.

While this is not a workbook, it nonetheless should be a learning companion when practicing the skills taught to you by your golf pro. For quite a while don't leave home for the driving range without it. Treat it as a learning manual to help you use your mind and emotions to get what you want. Read

Part 1 carefully and do the exercises presented there. This will make the rest of the book more meaningful. After doing the Sherlock Holmes Exercise and learning how to "anchor" your internal resources, read Part 2 casually. Then study and use the appropriate techniques in Part 2 when something in your game, or temperament, needs to be retuned or cleared up.

Not every lesson is for you. The final chapter, "The 19th Hole," contains information about how to identify your outcomes and guides you in selecting appropriate metaskills techniques to achieve them. However, I encourage you only to pay attention to the crucial elements of your swing you want to improve. I'm a firm believer in the notion, "If it ain't broke, don't fix it."

Setting aside mental-practice time is essential for learning my metaskills techniques. Merely *reading* this book is not enough to determine its effectiveness. *Do only one exercise at a time.* Learn how it works and determine if it fits your mental style. Judge for yourself the validity of a technique in relation to the quality of your performance and the degree to which you achieve each specific outcome.

My writing partner, whose love of golf once compelled him to play nine holes in Scotland while waiting for a rental car, experienced brainlock trying to use too many of my exercises at once. He learned, the hard way, the importance of exploring one technique at a time. The less you think about while swinging, the better your performance.

What eventually became useful for Ken was the concept of effort control described in Chapter 8. He applies that concept to lag-putting and those short putts which, when missed, can result in putters flying through the air like helicopter blades. The most valuable parts of the book for him were the ones that dealt with performance expectations and mood changes.

Which ones will be most useful for you? Happy exploring.

I

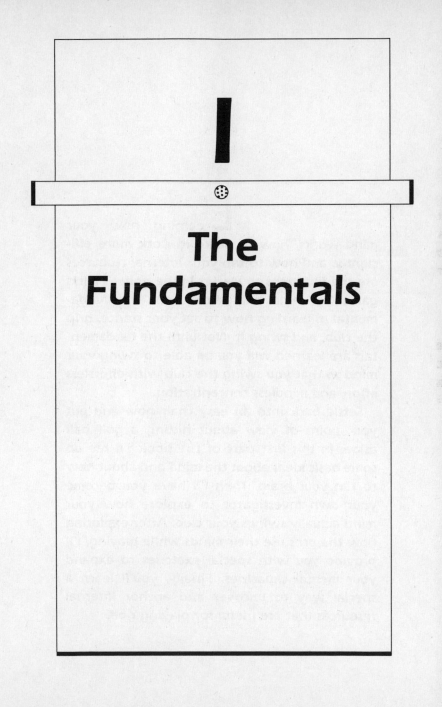

The Fundamentals

Learning how your mind works, how to make it work more efficiently, and how to tap your internal resources are the first steps to master in the golfer's mind game. The initial part of this book is as fundamental as learning how to set your stance, grip the club, and swing it. Not until the fundamentals are learned will you be able to swing your mind so that you swing the club with effortless effort and mindless concentration.

Settle back into an easy chair now and put your point of view about hitting a golf ball aside. In this first part of the book I'll tee up some basic ideas about the mind and about how to run your brain. Then I'll have you become your own investigator to explore how your mind actually swings your club. After exploring how the pros use their minds while playing, I'll provide you with special exercises to expand your mental capacities. Finally, you'll learn a special way to uncover and anchor internal resources that are useful for playing golf.

ONE

Teeing It Up

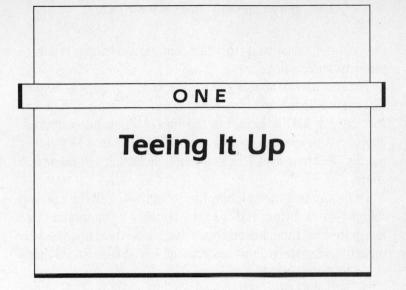

Ted Jackson was an eighty-two-year-old golfer with a problem as common—and frustrating—as a cold. He would maneuver his shots well enough until the cup was about the length of a football field away. From ninety-plus yards his ball was an unguided missile, skittering into deep rough, thwacking off trees, flying every which way but straight.

A few years ago Ted uttered two words familiar to me and to everyone else for whom sport has gone sour: "What's wrong?"

Answering a question like that isn't very useful because it can reinforce his mistakes. So I focused on the solution instead of on the problem.

I asked him, "Have you ever in your life hit a ninety-yard pitch shot well?" Of course, he had.

I told him to recreate that beautifully played shot in as much detail as possible. Was the day pleasant or overcast? How did the swing look and feel? Could he recall the sound of the *click* as he connected with the ball? Then I put him through a series of exercises, on the practice range and on the course, designed to train his unconscious mind to perform automatically.

Ted had known all along how to hit that shot. I was helping him realize that—and also never again to misplace it. I find that once a skill is locked in the mind, it can be retrieved, appropriately enough, with a key. Ted found that key rather quickly, and now uses it before routinely hitting splendid pitch shots.

Ted's key was a metaphor, the thought—of all the craziest things—of a flying red goose. It was a metaphor that integrated his thoughts and body and allowed his unconscious mind to swing the club so that the ball would consistently plop close to the flagstick.

How Ted created his metaphor will be fully explained in a subsequent chapter. For now, it's only important to realize that all the mind games in this book reflect Ted's experience. They are unusual and fun; and they work.

They're based on a couple of very simple and basic ideas: the unity of mind and body and the power of the unconscious mind.

Mind-Body Unity

The fundamental principle underlying my perspective of human behavior in general, and athletic performance in particular, is that mind, body, and emotion are integrated—inextricably interwoven. It's sort of like having your two hands pressed together as one, gripping the club.

Thought influences feelings and performance; feelings affect thought and performance; and performance affects thought and feelings. Specifically, the quality and consistency of an athlete's performance depends upon *how* he thinks and *how* he feels emotionally.

The metaskills techniques presented in this book are designed to affect your thought processes and emotional states, with only minimal attention to the content of your thoughts.

The Unconscious Mind in Sports

Think about thinking. It's usually detrimental in sports because it destroys concentration, a goal of most golfers. As in Zen meditation, the ideal state of concentration is to pay attention to nothing. This is also true when swinging a golf club. But this is an extremely difficult task. The next best way of thinking is to pay attention to *only one thing.* It might be watching the ball, feeling your grip, hearing a phrase in your head, or seeing an image in your mind's eye, whatever works for you.

For instance, if airborne Mary Lou Retton had to mentally process every bit of information necessary to execute that perfect-vaulting ten in the 1984 Olympics—feet together at takeoff . . . hands exactly so to get into the twist . . . knees bent at a precise moment in the air—she would never have landed on a Wheaties box.

Instead, Mary Lou tied every bit of complex movement into a single anchor. That anchor was one word: *stick.* She knew unconsciously what was necessary, in the air, to achieve perfection, to "stick" a ten and to "stick" to the mat after a flawless trip. That word triggered her unconscious mind, which automatically guided her body to achieve Olympian power and grace.

I know the paramount role the unconscious mind has in affecting human behavior. Superb athletic performance is regulated with little or no conscious thought given to purpose and mechanics. The clichés that reinforce this are numerous: "paralysis by analysis," "playing in the zone," and "It's like I wasn't there."

Conscious processing is entirely too slow and results in confusion. You don't think about hitting a baseball; you just do it. If you thought about how to connect with a slider, low and outside, the umpire would have his thumb jerked in the air for strike three before the bat got off your shoulder.

The more refined the athlete's performance, the more the unconscious mind is in control. While conscious attention to performance is most important during learning and practice, mindless (unconscious) processes regulate exquisite execution of skills already mastered.

Neuro-Linguistic Programming

During the past fifteen years a new psychotechnology has emerged on the scene. It's called Neuro-Linguistic Programming (NLP), and was created by Richard Bandler and John Grinder. It is essentially a multipurpose technology of communication that is used to identify how people actually regulate their behavior with their minds. It is used to help people change their behavior rather quickly by changing mental processes. NLP is one of the bases of my work, along with cognitive psychology.

In my opinion NLP is one of the most useful, and perhaps the most powerful psychological tool for helping people change. It's state-of-the-art theory and practice based on verbal and nonverbal communication processes. Increasing numbers of psychologists and psychiatrists are coming to recognize its usefulness. In case you're interested, there's a selected list of references in the back of the book.

The elements of the NLP model that apply to golf are *information processing, mental strategies, emotional states,* and *beliefs and values.*

Information Processing and Mental Strategies

Let's look a little closer at the way your golfing mind works. How does someone know how to swing a golf club, drive a car, or do anything, for that matter? By reproducing in his mind the sights, sounds, feelings, smell, and tastes associated with how he did it in the past.

In a span of two or three seconds—the time it takes to swing a golf club—we will unconsciously process as many as a hundred bits of patterned, or programed, sensory information—sights, sounds, and feelings—to control our behavior. This programed information, or strategy, fires off just nanoseconds in advance of a behavior such as sinking a seven-foot putt. If the golfer's putting program is wrong or is interrupted, he gets the "yips."

The mental programing we've developed for ourselves over a lifetime is much more sophisticated than anything that could be put on a floppy disk. And the nice thing about our programs is that they're flexible. We can change them at a moment's notice when we sense, consciously or unconsciously, that they ought to be altered for our own best interests.

We often find several separate strategies in operation to regulate a number of different behaviors at the same time. For example, consider a figure skater who falls while doing her free-skating program. First, she must initiate her decision-making strategy to determine if she will continue skating. If she decides to continue, her motivation strategy is energized to carry out that decision.

Since the present situation (falling) is not exactly like any previous instance, she sets her creativity strategy in motion to put together the necessary movements to get her back in time with the music and the planned routine. Knowing where she ought to be in the planned program also requires that her memory strategy be set off. To actually perform the new movements that will get her back to a point where she can move her body and limbs to match the movements of her program, she activates her performance strategy.

Whew!

Within several seconds, or much less time that it took you to read this, she triggered five separate strategies: *decision-making, motivation, creativity, memory,* and *performance.* Each strategy was somewhat dependent upon the others. Unconscious thought, that which is out of awareness, was much more significant for her athletic performance than conscious thought. And the more streamlined the mental process, the faster her reaction time—or that of any athlete.

Although golfers have more time to think about their shots, they, too, go through the same kinds of mental processes quickly, and often unconsciously, when they prepare to hit a ball. Consider an errant shot that strays into the woods and becomes ensnarled in twigs and leaves under a low-hanging branch. Under these conditions the golfer must: *decide* how to stand and swing, based on his *memory* of similar shots and his ability to *create* the appropriate stance for the situation at hand; *motivate* himself to hit the ball with deep concentration; and then actually *perform,* executing the shot as planned.

This complex form of mentally regulating human behavior is called a cybernetic system. Feed-forward and feedback mechanisms are constantly in operation as the athlete performs, usually out of conscious awareness. The internal regulatory systems of the body are constantly comparing ongoing internal and external sensory data with the output of the muscles that bring about our intended behavior, like hitting a golf ball.

Let's say you're standing on the tee of a par 3, 175-yard hole with about 160 of those yards across a pond. Information about where you would like the ball to land, how you want to be set up to the ball, and how to swing is fed forward into the entire operation of planning and executing the tee shot. Information about how the club actually feels in your hands, the actual alignment of the club face, the stability of your stance, the smoothness of the swing itself, and certain important environmental information, like the wind, is constantly being fed back to your mind, either in or out of your awareness.

Comparisons are continuously and rapidly being made in your brain, consciously and unconsciously, between information that is fed forward and information that is fed back. When the comparisons match, no change in the operation of the system is initiated. *Voilà!* You tee up the ball, plan the shot over the pond, make a silky pass, and the ball lands five feet from the pin. Your unconscious mind is so sensitive, it makes your reaction and adjustment during takeaway to an unexpected breeze a breeze.

Metaskills techniques are designed to affect the basic elements of the golfer's mental strategies, especially the internal comparison processes he uses to evaluate his swing. The techniques are designed to change or stabilize a golfer's performance by changing how he thinks—how he processes sights, sounds, feelings, smells, and tastes in his mind.

Just-Right Emotional State

Although people's programed mental strategies for hitting golf balls are different, what's common to all of us is the fact that we must be in an appropriate mood or emotional state for a particular strategy to be activated. And each of us has unique just-right states for accomplishing different tasks. When you are in the just-right state for a particular task, the patterned sequence of all of the auditory, visual, and kinesthetic information that represents your experience of having done that task before is automatically and unconsciously fired off before and during the execution of that task. However, if you're not in the right state, the strategy for the task will be defective because key elements in it will be missing.

I'm sure you know that the state you want to be in while going for a six-foot downhill breaking putt on a slick green will be much different from the state you want to be in when you take that 175-yard drive over water. On the one hand you want a delicate touch; on the other you want to muster the power needed to prevent a splash.

Because of the centrality of the emotions, many of my metaskills techniques are based on identifying and anchoring the appropriate internal states for hitting different golf shots. When they're properly anchored, the swing will be executed automatically. Getting into those just-right states is part of what this book is about.

Beliefs and Values

Golfers can't leave their beliefs and values behind when they head out to the course. A belief is something accepted as true without certainty of proof; a value is something important to each individual, and serves as a guide to making decisions. They are at work during every golf game, affecting the golfer's moods from moment to moment. Since moods influence mental strategies, beliefs and values either facilitate or intrude on what could be very pleasurable.

Compare the emotional responses of two different golfers

when down three holes with four to play. One golfer values winning and perfection and believes victory should be based on expert performance. If he has made a lot of bad shots, his emotional response will most probably be dejection; he thinks he doesn't deserve to win, playing as badly as he has.

Another player, however, might respond positively to the same situation; his attitude could be that here is an unprecedented chance to learn what has prevented him from playing up to his potential. The first player is controlled by values pertaining to perfection and winning; the second, in exactly the same context, is influenced by his belief in the value of any experience being an opportunity to learn and change.

The first player is dejected, the second curious and optimistic. The chances of the second player winning the match are certainly higher than for the first player because his emotional state, influenced by his beliefs and values, is more conducive to good play.

In many instances changing beliefs and reordering your values can affect your performance. This book will help you do just that.

Communication and Change

The techniques in this book are forms of communication that are intended to change your behavior. They are designed to influence your mental strategies, emotional states, and your beliefs and values. My instructions are deliberately intended to affect the *way* you perceive the environment and the *way* you communicate with yourself—the *way* you run your brain. Your attention will be limited to how you process relevant sights, sounds, and feelings, not to how you address, swing, and hit the ball. My techniques do not teach you the proper physical mechanics of addressing the ball and of holding and swinging the club; that's the golf pro's job. However, while you are learning the mechanics of golf, or after you have learned them, my mental techniques will help you execute them better.

Self-hypnosis

Some of my exercises are based on hypnosis because it is a mental state that permits the golfer to access important information within himself about hitting golf balls and because a hypnotic state is a mental characteristic of fine performance. Although highly sophisticated daydreaming might be as good a way to describe some of what actually happens during a hypnotic state, my work is Walter Mitty stuff, nothing scary. Most athletes, in fact, are in a trance, a profound altered state, when they perform superbly.

Admit it, now. You've transformed yourself, perhaps at a traffic light or at the office, to the 18th tee at Augusta National, needing only a routine par for Jack Nicklaus to help you slip into something worthy of a legend. Make that green jacket a 44 regular! In your mind you see the flawless swing that just might get that accomplished, the one that made you most proud on your home course.

Growing up, you watched Sandy Koufax, Arnold Palmer, Billie Jean King, and other wondrous athletes. Later you tried to mimic their seemingly unique motions in your mind—and then scooted outside and worked on duplicating them. What surely never entered your mind at the time is that you were using a kind of self-hypnosis. I have techniques that use that concept, one of which can make your putting stroke seem a whole lot like Ben Crenshaw's.

I was working one afternoon with George Burns, the touring pro, at his club. He has been playing so long, there are few situations where he can't recall having hit a fine shot somewhere in similar circumstances. But on one hole George couldn't remember ever having been faced with a particular shot. So I said, "Have you ever seen anyone else hit one like that?"

Out of thin air he grabbed a golfing god.

"Nicklaus. I saw Nicklaus hit that shot."

We then began a process I'll explain in full later, in which George pictured Nicklaus hitting the shot. And then, in his mind, he pictured himself hitting the shot as if he were Nicklaus. Finally, George struck the ball, and it landed a few feet from the pin. That process took no more than five minutes, and George was in an altered state during much of that time.

What Will This Book Do for You?

The metaskills techniques will improve your golf game by changing the way you think and feel. You'll learn how your mind regulates your golf swing. You'll learn how to expand and modify your sensory apparatus so your thinking is changed. You'll learn how your emotions can be controlled so your mind can work smoothly and unconsciously; you'll learn how to use self-hypnosis to identify your mental resources. In short, you'll learn to have more choices about how to hit a golf ball so that your golf game improves and your sense of enjoyment is enhanced.

If you're a 90-shooter, these techniques won't get you an invitation to the Masters. Still, they'll get you out of bunkers more quickly, if that's a goal, or get you to hit higher and longer shots off the fairway. Using them will make you as fine at specific skills as your ability allows, and better able to cope with such miseries as knee-knocker putts.

This book will help you get in the just-right state so your mental golf-shot programs will take over. You'll learn to get your conscious mind out of the way, stop talking to yourself, stop doing anything, and just let go when you swing.

How to Use This Book

Use this book to supplement the work of your golf pro whose job it is to teach you the actual mechanics of golf. You can read it whenever you have a spare moment and refer to it during your practice sessions.

The time frame for learning any one of the techniques can range from half an hour to a few weeks. It all depends on what you want, and how much energy you give to getting it. Practice for the mind also takes time.

I can't emphasize often enough that the best way to learn my techniques is to experience them first hand while *doing* something—lag putting, for instance, or regulating your swing tempo—something very precise that you would like to improve. First find out what happens to the way you play golf; analyze and evaluate the usefulness of a technique in terms of your improvement, not in terms of whether my approach fits existing psychological theory.

The goal is to have your unconscious mind in complete control during competition. Seldom will there be a need for conscious application of any metaskills techniques while playing a match. If you've learned them well, they'll take over automatically, just as your ideal golf swing follows a grooved pattern.

The essence of my approach and the way I want you to use this book was best expressed in *Golf in the Kingdom* by Michael Murphy:

> "But this is the thing," he raised his hand and shook a finger at me, "ye can only know wha' it is by livin' into it yersel'—not through squeezin' it and shovin' it the way they do in the universities and laboratories. Ye must go into the heart o' it, through yer own body and senses and livin' experience, level after level *right to the heart o' it.* Ye see, Michael, merely shootin' par is second best. Goin' for results like that leads men and cultures and entire worlds astray. But if ye do it from the inside ye get the results eventually and *everythin' else along with it.* So ye will na' see me givin' people many tips about the gowf swings lik' they do in all the 'how-to' books. I will na' do it. Ye must start from the inside, lik' I showed ye there." *

Controlling your golf swing, indeed, comes from the inside out, first consciously, then unconsciously. Your beliefs and values, your emotions and your thought processes, regulate the quality of your swing and the extent of your enjoyment. My metaskills techniques are based on tapping your unconscious resources through your senses—going "right to the heart o' it"—and getting your conscious mind out of your way.

Let's get started.

Published by the Viking Press (New York, 1972), pp. 85–86; reprint Delta Books (New York: Dell Publishing, 1973).

TWO

The Sherlock Holmes Exercise: Discover How Your Mind Regulates Your Golf Shots

This is a must-read chapter; it's fundamental to everything that follows. Practically all of the techniques in this book deal with "going inside" and retrieving past experiences. These remembered experiences are resources to be used to refine your game. How to go about doing that is what you'll learn in this chapter.

Be Sherlock Holmes for a while and discover the important elements of your setup and swing. Knowing about them will help you become more consistent, if you're already a sweet swinger. Being able to find them, on command, is essential to playing my unique mind games.

All you have to think about is being wonderful, in your own mind, at least. As Sherlock you'll be searching for clues that make your performance so special. It's important that you go to a quiet place to do this exercise. When you do, you will recall when you played a particular shot exceptionally well and relive it in exquisite detail. You'll think about a very specific shot, not an entire round, or even a whole hole. Out of the hundreds or thousands of shots you've struck, you'll simply select one shot that made you proud. Maybe it was a tee shot that split the fairway, or an approach hit stiff to the pin, or a long, breaking putt that dropped for a birdie.

The idea is to uncover some of the crucial elements of the mental sequence, or strategy, that regulates your movements. That strategy contains a series of representations of sensory cues—sights, sounds, and feelings. I use the letters *V, A,* and *K* to signify those cues; *V* is for visual, *A* is for auditory, and *K* is for kinesthetic—muscle and joint feelings, feelings on the surface of your body, and the bodily sensations associated with emotions.

During the execution of a three-second golf swing, from take-away to follow-through, your mind processes as many as one hundred bits of sensory information with machine-gun rapidity. Just a few of those sensory representations are in your conscious awareness. The rest are processed unconsciously because of the speed of the swing.

Sensory information consists of specific internal sights, sounds, and feelings representing specific, *past* experiences of swinging the golf club along with *ongoing,* internal and external sights, sounds, and feelings that are occurring as you swing.

Here's how I want you to think about that specific golf shot. First, just do a general, overall review of it, like watching a sound movie. *See* the course where you were playing, the lie of the ball, the distance to the pin. Notice the light and shadows and the brightness of the colors. See the images that were in your mind as you were taking that shot. Maybe you were imagining the flight of the ball.

Hear again what you heard then, both on the outside and inside your mind. Perhaps you heard the *whoosh* of your club and the sound of your own voice giving yourself instructions. Pay attention to the loudness and pitch and tempo of those sounds. As you see and hear those things, *feel* again what you felt then during your setup and swing—the coordinated movements of your body and the tension and relaxation of your muscles. Also, become aware of the mood or emotional state you were in as you were swinging and hitting the ball.

Now it's time to get out Holmes's magnifying glass and ear trumpet and pay more attention to the details of what you saw, heard, and felt back then, on the outside and inside your mind. The main questions to ask yourself as you relive that shot again and again in detail are these: What were the things you saw, the things you heard, and the things you felt that let you know when and how to swing the club? What did you see, hear, and feel that let you know that your movements were either okay or needed to be corrected?

You're looking for clues in this exercise, details that control what you already know how to do, but may not know that you know. Sometime during the exercise, for instance, you might notice that you took the club all the way back to parallel. That is a clue. The more clues you can gather, the better your swing will become.

Forget about spectators and forget about what your playing partners did. Just pay attention to the sensory clues—what you saw, heard, and felt—that regulated your shot. Those clues could be related to your alignment, stance, grip, or swing and the mood or state you were in.

Make mental notes of your clues as you go along. At the end of the search you can write down what's important.

The way you watch your past performance, the way you listen to the sounds associated with it, and the kind of bodily sensations that you pay attention to will determine your success as Sherlock Holmes. The more thorough you are, the better clues you will uncover.

Identifying the V's—the Sights

First pay attention to what you saw on the outside as if you were right there on the course, standing over the ball and making that shot. I call these images "regular" pictures. Then shift your way of watching so that you see yourself hitting the golf ball. It might be helpful to imagine stepping out of your body, walking a few paces, and then turning to gaze upon a piece of athletic magic about to unfold from your favorite athletic star—you.

From this visual perspective, called the "meta position," take the role of Sherlock Holmes and search for something that you didn't know you knew that made your golf shot so good.

As you watch yourself perform, change the image of yourself—the *meta picture*—to color if it is black and white; change it to black and white if it is in color. If the picture is bright, make it dull; if it is dull, make it bright. If the picture is sharply defined, make it fuzzy; if fuzzy, make it defined. Notice what happens to the quality of your performance as you vary the internal images this way; your performance may get better or worse. Does your swing get better or worse as you vary the color, brightness, focus, and size of the images? Make mental notes about the kinds of images that made your performance good.

Now make regular pictures of your setup and swing, no longer watching yourself. See again what you saw while setting up and swinging. Vary the color, brightness, and definition of what you saw as you were striking the ball. Continue to search for the important clues that let you know when and how to swing. Look for the clues that let you know whether your movements were okay or needed to be changed. Notice what happens to the quality of your swing as you vary the images. Does it improve or deteriorate?

Now take a moment to become aware of the internal images, the ones you had in your mind then, when you were swinging the club. What were they, if any? For example, did you see an image of the proper grip? Did you see an imaginary line in front of the ball directing you to the target? How were these internal images helpful?

Identifying the A's—the Sounds

While watching your past performance, using either regular or meta pictures, hear again what you heard then. Listen to the sounds directly associated with setting up and swinging. Listen to the sounds in the surrounding environment and the sounds in your mind. For instance, on the outside you might hear your spikes striking the ground as you set up to the ball, or the breeze in nearby trees. On the inside, in your mind, you might hear silence or your own voice giving yourself instructions.

If the sounds were loud, make them barely audible; if hardly heard, turn up the volume. If they were high-pitched tones, make them low; if low-pitched, make them high. If they were harmonious, make them discordant and unpleasant; if unpleasant, make them harmonious. If the tempo of the sounds was an even beat, make it irregular; if irregular, make it even. And while you're varying the sounds, notice if the quality of your performance improves or deteriorates. Continue, as Sherlock Holmes, to listen for the important clues that were present when your movements were just like they were supposed to be. Are some sounds more important than others? Make a mental note of your discoveries.

Identifying the K's—the Bodily Sensations

As you relive hitting the shot over and over again, pay close attention to: (1) the feelings of your coordinated movements, (2) the feelings of certain parts of your body that were essential to setting up and swinging, (3) the amount of energy and tension you felt in your muscles, and (4) the bodily feelings that represented the mood you were in while you were hitting the ball.

There might be a number of things you could feel as you do this exercise. For instance, you might feel the turn of your shoulders on the backswing, or the strength of your grip on the club, or the lifting of your forward heel toward the end of the backswing.

Now, in your mind, vary the way you moved. If your movements were quick, slow them down; if slow, speed them up. If you were exerting a lot of energy and pressure, relax the effort; if you weren't, increase the tension of your muscles. While varying those feelings, notice what happens to the quality of your performance. Does your swing get better or worse? As Sherlock Holmes, continue to identify and make mental notes of the feelings that made your performance so good.

Equally as important as the muscular feelings that were associated with setting up and swinging the club are the emotional feelings you had *while,* not after, you were actually hitting the ball. Those bodily sensations represent the mood or state you were in. Feel them again. Perhaps they were feelings of lightness, fluttering, tingling, warmth, tension, or pulsing that were present in parts of your body. Vary the intensity of these emotional feelings and find out what happens to the quality of the shot. Does it get better or worse when you increase or decrease the intensity? What is the amount of intensity that is just right for making that shot the best possible?

Putting It All Together

After you've gone through seeing, listening, and feeling, have some fun with reliving that past performance. Pretend you've got a videotape of it, and watch it while using the variable speed and direction buttons on the video control.

First, run the tape twice as fast as normal, then four times as fast, and then bring the speed back to normal. In addition, slow the tape down to half speed and then to one frame at a time. Be sure to bring the tape back up to normal speed. With each variation in speed carefully pay attention, as before, to discovering new visual, auditory, and kinesthetic clues that were essential for hitting the ball so well.

Now run the tape in reverse—in normal, slow, and fast motion—again looking for clues. Finish up by running the tape forward again, analyzing and evaluating your performance in light of what you've discovered.

Before reading any further, go through the entire Sherlock Holmes Exercise now.

SHERLOCK HOLMES EXERCISE

1. Go to a quiet room. With experience you'll be able to do it out on the practice range or course.
2. Remember a specific shot that you hit during a round.
3. See everything you can see about the shot; hear everything you can hear about the shot; feel everything you can feel about the shot.
4. Vary what you see (from color to black and white, from fuzzy to clear); change the sounds (from loud to soft, from pleasant to unpleasant); alter your feelings from relaxed to tense).
5. Remember the details. Write them down if it'll help. Judge what seems most important.

Reactions to the Sherlock Holmes Exercise

Although there are some typical sensory cues that most golfers pay attention to while they're making a shot, each person has his or her own way of processing and giving meaning to sensory information. There are no right or wrong sensory cues for playing golf. It's what you do with them that's important.

To help you understand how professional golfers process

information, I'll share with you what I learned from some of them when they did the Sherlock Holmes Exercise. Their mental processes are often unusual and quite sophisticated.

What the Pros See—the Internal V's

Former U.S. Open and PGA Champion David Graham sees images of past shots as he decides how to make the shot facing him.

Touring pro Danny Edwards checks his setup as if he is facing himself. For a second or two he mentally steps outside his body, almost into the gallery, and looks back. When Danny is convinced that everything about his setup is okay from that perspective, he hops back inside and lets the ball fly. Lon Hinkle, another PGA Tour professional, makes pictures of himself properly set up and swinging from behind the ball. He then walks up to the ball and "steps into" his created pictures.

When Bill Burgess, 1987 Nissan Classic Champion and head club professional at Arcola Country Club in Paramus, New Jersey, played investigator, he found he had an image of strings that connect his ball with the target. He described it "as if there were strings out there, lines. And it felt like everything matched up to the lines, so all I had to do was swing the club. I can't always do it. But when I can get the strings and feel the lines, I always hit good shots."

All pros that I've talked to imagine the actual trajectory they want the ball to follow before striking it. They know precisely where they want the ball to come to rest, either in the fairway, or in the hole on putts.

What the Pros Hear—the Internal A's

The internal auditory information of professional golfers almost always consists of short, positive statements or commands. Peter Jacobsen routinely says to himself, "Knock it close." David Graham says, "Rhythm," as he approaches the ball, and he repeats the phrase "Good shot" throughout his backswing.

Mike Davis, a colleague of Bill Burgess at Arcola, quickly calls off in his mind a checklist of the key elements of his setup and swing as a part of his preshot mental routine. Mike Sparks, an assistant pro at Ridgewood Country Club in New Jersey, listens to music in his head when he's in his best playing mood.

"I never realized it," he said, "but when I replayed my shot and heard what was in my head, I learned I sing a song to myself. Before I hit shots, I get in a mode where I kind of do my own deal and don't pay attention to people. Maybe it's a tune I've heard in the car on the way to the course that day."

Bill Loeffler, a former PGA Tour professional, and Mike McCullough, currently on tour, both "hear" silence as a positive indication that they're ready to hit the ball well.

What the Pros Feel—the Internal K's

The way golfers feel emotionally on the inside is absolutely crucial for playing golf consistently well. As you might expect, Sherlock Holmes revealed that the emotional state most conducive for good play varies from person to person and from time to time. Mike Davis says he feels relaxed when he plays well. Bill Burgess says, "Instead of feeling relaxed like Mike, I feel slightly juiced up in my legs and arms. When I get turned up a notch, I really play better."

Another touring craftsman, George Burns, says, "I have a

feeling of freedom in my chest, belly, arms, and shoulders when I'm on my game." And Bill Adams, head pro at Ridgewood, has "a feeling of eagerness" in his forearms that lets him know that it's time to putt, and a "loosey-goosey feeling" when he's ready to chip.

Identifying the just-right states—the emotional K's—for hitting various golf shots is perhaps the most important set of internal clues that you can identify; and the ability to quickly generate that state at will is undoubtedly the most important skill you can learn. Chapters 4, 5, and 6 are devoted to this important process.

External, or "Uptime" Cues

The kinds of sensory cues that pros identified while doing the Sherlock Holmes Exercise have been, up to this point, "internal" cues—what they saw, heard, and felt inside of themselves; I refer to them as "downtime" cues. Now I want to briefly identify what the pros saw, heard, and felt on the outside—the important sensations that come directly from the environment or are associated directly with the movements that control their golf swings. As you might expect, I refer to these environmental and movement sensations as "uptime" cues. An extensive list of what good golfers consider to be the most important "uptime" cues can be found in Appendix A.

Uptime *visual* cues that pros attend to are familiar to you, I'm sure, because most golfers are sensitive to them. They include: location of the target and intervening hazards, out-of-bounds markers, contours of the fairway and green, alignment of the body with respect to the target, and, of course, the lie of the ball.

The significant uptime *auditory* cues that pros listen to are: the wind, the *whoosh* of the club on the downswing, the *click* of the ball coming off the club head, and their breathing. Chip

Beck, one of the elite golfers on the PGA Tour, uses the sound of his spikes as he walks up to the ball. This helps him determine how big a divot he wants to take on approach shots. He combines this with the feel of the grass underfoot to make that decision.

The most important uptime *kinesthetic* cues of most pros are associated with the grip, stance, and swing mechanics. Lee Trevino feels his grip on the club as if he's holding a bird in his hands. Bob Tosky, a master golf teacher, has the sensation of accelerating the clubhead speed at the bottom of the swing. Mike Davis feels increased tension in his hands and wrists when his club head is about a foot from the ball on the downswing.

Some Important Questions and Answers

Since the price of this book does not include me, I've anticipated some of the questions the Sherlock Holmes Exercise might inspire.

Q. What am I supposed to see, hear, and feel?

A. Whatever you *do* see, hear, and feel. Each one of us has developed our own set of clues that regulate our behavior; some have more clues to good performance than others. Also, some people become so involved as Sherlock, they think they're actually on the course. So don't go into this exercise with preconceived ideas.

Q. How come you had me change what I saw, heard, and felt so often? Why change colors to black and white and then back? Why change the tension in my muscles? Why change the volume of the sound?

A. Technically, I'm dealing with what we call sensory submodalities. Modalities are seeing, hearing, and feeling. As you know, there are also the modalities of smelling and tasting, but they're of little consequence for our purposes. Submodalities are the refined elements of seeing, hearing, and feeling such as color, volume, and tension. Without getting too complex, mentally varying the submodalities of sight, sound, and feeling is when learning—and change—occur. Trust me.

Q. Was I in a trance?

A. You could call it that. You changed into a different state when you were asked to relive a past shot. Most athletes are in a trance—a profound altered state—when they perform superbly.

Q. Will I be learning hypnosis?

A. Actually, you know how to do it already. I'll be telling you how to use self-hypnosis in Chapter 9.

Now that you know how to retrieve the details of past experience, let's start playing some of my mind games so your golf game improves. If after doing the Sherlock Holmes Exercise you have difficulty with generating images in your mind, with making internal sounds, or with feeling a variety of physical sensations, you can use the questions and exercises in Appendix B to expand or refine your sensory awareness. The better that is, the easier it will be for you to apply metaskills techniques.

THREE

Anchoring: Tapping Your Inner Resources

This chapter is your guide to making the most of your past experience. Here you'll learn how to identify the kinds of internal mental and emotional resources you have within you to play better golf, and then how to make them automatically available for eventual application on the golf course.

As you know, golf is essentially a mental game, because there's so much time to think in between shots. The actual act of setting up to the ball and striking it takes twenty-five to thirty seconds. If you play a round in par, it means that you're spending about thirty minutes out of four and a half hours actively playing the game. Thirteen minutes per hole is spent walking or riding, talking, and, of course, thinking between shots.

It's those between-shot periods that can jump up and jostle a golfer's mind. They can tense the muscles, decrease concentration, cause forgetfulness, reduce confidence, and eventually produce inconsistent shots—unless he or she knows how to keep focused on the here and now.

What is needed, then, is a way to keep yourself in the

proper frame of mind between shots; that is, to be in the appropriate emotional state when you're ready to hit the ball. The appropriate states of mind needed to play good golf vary from person to person and situation to situation, depending perhaps upon the lie of the ball, your score, and the pace of play.

Not only do conditions on the course affect your state, but whatever is on your mind—your business, your school, your family, or your social life—also affects your game. The capacity to leave outside interests out of your mind while playing is crucial if you want to play well consistently. The states you generate on the course that keep you attentive to the present moment are what count.

There are three underlying states of mind that are essential to playing well consistently. They are concentration, confidence, and a sense of mind-body unity. As you probably know, playing good golf requires riveted concentration on the shot at hand. When not concentrating, many golfers get ahead of themselves, imagining that they are on the next tee or in the clubhouse having shot a preconceived score. They forget that they still have a shot to make and more holes to play.

Confidence of your ability to execute a planned shot well is necessary if you want to play to your handicap or better. While in this state you know that a shot will be good even before you strike the ball. But if there's doubt in your mind, shots start to fly all over the place.

As a result of concentration and confidence, you will develop an inner sense of unity. This state of mind has elements of resonance and harmony, rhythmic energy, and grooved coordinated movement that feels effortless. When in this state—some call it a "zone"—golfers sense that their mind, mood, and movement are all-of-a-piece, resulting in shots that are "pure."

As you will see in Chapters 4, 5, and 6, there are a variety of metaskills techniques that facilitate the development and maintenance of these three states. But for now we will focus on general procedures to identify and retrieve specific internal resources that will make for more consistent play.

Your Inner Resources

You've done a lot of living and have all sorts of experiences stored in your memory that can be used to generate appropriate states of mind for playing good golf. These "resource states" include, among others, optimism, eagerness, determination, calmness, inventiveness, hopefulness, acceptance, patience, friendliness, sensitivity to nature, and a lot more. Optimism helps you to think positively about your shots; eagerness and determination keep you focused on the shot at hand; calmness keeps your swing fluid; inventiveness and hope are needed to create new shots to get out of trouble; patience and friendliness allow you to overlook the slowness and perhaps golfing ignorance of your playing partners; and sensitivity to the beauty of nature around you can be a counterpoint to much of the anxiety in your life, on or off the course.

Other useful resources include past experiences related to learning all sorts of physical skills; embedded in these experiences are the basic resources for playing golf well, such as balance, power, strength, energy, rhythm, coordination, and effort control. Finally, your past experiences of making good golf shots contain unconscious mental strategies, the resources that directly control your game.

Identifying the Right Resources

By now you've probably assumed that you're about to learn to put yourself into the right frame of mind—confident, optimistic, patient—at will. But first you must decide *which* resource to call up from your past experience. You'll know this by answering two basic questions: (1) "Specifically, what kind of shots do I want to make?" and (2) "What stops me from hitting the ball the way I want to hit it or the way I'm capable of hitting it?" Let's look at the answers to these two questions, one at a time.

To answer the first question, knowing what you want comes from having alternatives in mind. These alternatives include remembering precisely when and how you've hit similar shots in the past, remembering how other good golfers have executed similar shots, or recalling instructions from your pro. This means knowing what you would have to see, hear, and feel for the shot to be good. Then you can transfer pertinent information to the shot facing you at the moment.

Frequently, the answer that some people give to the second question, "What stops me?" is "I don't know. If I did, I'd do something about it." Yet there are ways to uncover the answer to this question. One way is to guess. By guessing, you'll be tapping into your unconscious mind; and frequently guesses turn out to be quite accurate.

If you have no good guesses, take another approach. Replay in your mind what you're doing incorrectly and compare it to the way you want to swing, using your own past performance or someone else's performance as a standard for comparison. When you identify the differences between how you mentally regulate what you're doing and how you mentally regulate what you want to do, you'll have some important clues as to what's stopping you.

Frequently, it's your emotional state that stops you from playing good golf. If you change to a just-right emotional state, your grooved swing will return. By paying close attention to the mood you're in, you may have the answer to what's stopping you. Perhaps you have been annoyed, impatient, skeptical, despairing, feeling hopeless, whatever. After identifying this stopper state, all that's necessary is to replace it with its opposite.

This isn't always as easy as it might seem. Sometimes it may be impossible to discover all the factors that keep you from achieving your outcomes. You may need the help of a golf professional to refine the mechanics of your swing, or you may need the help of a skilled counselor to deal with unconscious conflicts; such conflicts could interfere with maintaining the mood you need to play well.

Nonetheless, knowing how to identify and use your internal resources is a valuable process in itself; so let's look at it now.

Accessing Internal Resources

Fortunately, NLP has formalized the normal human process of tapping past experiences and making them automatically available for use in present situations. The Sherlock Holmes Exercise is part of this process; you already know it. By reliving past experiences in full detail, you'll be pleasantly surprised to discover that you have more resources for playing better golf than you thought you had. When you discover this, you'll trust yourself more and you will build your self-confidence.

Anchoring is the part of the process which makes your internal resources—your past experiences and feelings, still available to you in your subconscious—automatically available to play better golf in spite of conditions that conspire to make the game difficult. Anchors keep your resources stabilized so your game can become more consistent and enjoyable. Let's turn to the process of anchoring in general. Later you'll learn how to use a variety of anchors for specific aspects of your game.

What Is an Anchor?

An anchor is either an internal or actual external sight, sound, feeling, smell, or taste—a stimulus—that triggers the sensory details associated with a particular past experience. For example, when you see an old photograph of yourself as a child, it usually stirs up memories of that time in your life. Similarly, when you see azaleas and dogwoods, you could think of the Augusta National. It's the same with a special song.

It's a fact that our conscious and unconscious thoughts—what we see, hear, feel, smell, and taste internally—directly affect our moods or internal emotional states. Consequently, we can become conditioned to respond emotionally in the same way over and over again whenever we generate a particular thought or whenever a particular stimulus is experienced. You vaguely remember hearing this from someone else, don't you? Yes, it was Pavlov who got the dog to salivate simply by ringing a bell.

Our lives are full of anchors, some of which have powerful effects. The sight of the American flag or the sound of "America the Beautiful" inspires deep feelings of patriotism in some people. Seeing a snake or spider can evoke intense fear in those who are phobic. The smell of popcorn stirs up the just-right kind of feelings in Peter Carruthers, 1984 Olympic pairs skater, that he says makes him skate his best. The thought of a past event—like sinking an eagle approach shot—can evoke the same feelings associated with it in the here and now.

Golfers have more anchors than the Sixth Fleet. Unfortunately, most of them are negative, similar to phobias. Teeing up on the first tee, for instance, is enough to create intense anxiety in many golfers. Even the thought of participating in a tournament can evoke discomfort in some people or arouse excited anticipation in others. Water hazards seem to evoke gloom or fear in some golfers, resulting in golf balls drowned with regularity. All an uncertain golfer has to do is to look at the water and *splash,* in goes an old substitute ball.

Other anchors consist of some form of compulsive, superstitious behavior. Superstitious anchors range from wearing certain pieces of jewelry or clothing for good luck to believing in a "trusty" club that is expected to produce a good shot every time, even though another club would be more suitable for the shot at hand.

All of these uncontrollable phobic responses and compulsive, ritualistic behaviors override the ability to make intelligent choices about your actions. Ritualistic behaviors create internal pressure and can distract you from absorbing important external information, such as the distance to the pin, the strength of the wind, or the contour of the fairway and green. Moreover, they interfere with the internal state that is most appropriate for executing a well-hit golf shot.

On the other hand, metaskills anchors automatically evoke good feelings, without the need for conscious thought; they will utilize your talents and emotional states so that you play well consistently. This will free you to enjoy the game, the scenery, and your playing companions.

Retrieving Past Experiences

Let's see how we can use the Sherlock Holmes Exercise to retrieve past experiences so they can be anchored for practical use while playing golf. In that exercise you learned how to go inside your mind and retrieve or remember a past experience. You learned how to run your brain by modifying sights, sounds, and feelings. And you identified the condition or state of consciousness when your mental thoughts, emotions, and muscles conspired to create as fine a golf shot as you had ever made.

This process of "going inside"—actively remembering what you saw, heard, and felt during a particular past experience—is, as I've said, central to practically all of my mind games, because it's there, in your brain and muscles, where you have all the resources you need to play golf as well as your physical condition and skills will allow, or to do anything else worth doing.

Sherlock Holmes Revisited

Let's revisit the Sherlock Holmes Exercise as a way to learn how to anchor. Quickly reread the instructions on page 23 of Chapter 2. When you've finished reading, go inside and go back to that wonderful shot that you examined as Sherlock Holmes before. See, hear, and feel again what you saw heard, and felt when you hit that shot. Be sure to make regular pictures, not meta pictures, because regular pictures elicit stronger feelings. Especially feel the emotions you felt *while* you were hitting it. Pay attention to the bodily sensations of that emotional state. Perhaps it's a tingling feeling, goose bumps, warmth, a rush of blood, a feeling of energy or power in some part of your body, or whatever.

Intensify these sensations until they're as strong as you can make them. As they get stronger, press one finger against any *one specific part of your body.* Increase the amount of finger pressure as the intensity of the emotional sensations increases; as they subside, reduce the amount of finger pressure. That's the anchor—a K-anchor—the pressure of your finger on a specific part of your body. The central idea is to associate the anchor with the emotional feeling.

When the emotional feeling is at its most intense level, let one, and only one, internal image associated with the shot flash *spontaneously* in your mind; then let one sound associated with the shot *spontaneously* pop into your head. The image and sound are also anchors—a V-anchor and an A-anchor. They should be directly and specifically related to the shot and not to golf in general.

Now let your mind go blank and come back to the present. Take a five- or ten-minute break from reading this book and do something else to distract your mind from what you have been reading. At the end of the break return to this place where you are presently reading.

Welcome back. Take a moment to determine the nature of the state you're in right now. After that press your finger on the exact same spot on your body when you were Sherlock. Hold the finger pressure for a full sixty seconds without reading any further than the end of this paragraph. Just pay attention to what happens inside, nothing else, and then return to the book when the sixty seconds are up.

Welcome back again. Are you thinking about the past good shot? Do you now see or hear what you saw or heard then? Do you now feel the same emotions you felt when you hit that shot? I'd be surprised if you aren't aware of some aspect of the shot, assuming you followed my instructions. If you reactivated some of the same feelings, images, or sounds associated with the shot, you have experienced how an anchor works. Within sixty seconds you changed your state.

Now, reflect on the meaning of this experience. Do you realize that you can change your state quickly, and therefore don't have to stay stuck in a lousy state? With a properly established anchor you have more choices about the way you want to feel, and you can activate any state automatically if your anchor is "contextualized."

Contextual Anchors

If an anchored resource is to be useful on the golf course, it must be contextualized; that is, the anchor should fire *automatically* without conscious thought in the context of a special situation when a particular resource is needed, not just at any old time or in any situation. If anxiety normally takes over on the first tee, then a confidence anchor could be triggered automatically just before you approach the teeing ground. If you want to keep your cool when duffers are ahead, then a calmness anchor could be activated automatically when you first see the duffers hacking around. If a delicate putt is required, then the anchored feeling of having a fine touch could be fired automatically as you study the line and distance to the cup.

When you contextualize an anchor, it's important to select either a movement, an *external* visual cue, or an *external* auditory cue that is always present on the golf course to serve as an anchor. Only one cue is necessary. For example, tying the laces of your golf shoes, a K-anchor, could be an anchor for generating the resource of determination; and looking at a tee marker, a V-anchor, could be used to get into the right state for making a tee shot.

Your ingenuity is all that's necessary to identify an anchor. Using a habitual movement that occurs in a particular situation or context as an anchor is most effective, since it already is unconsciously automatic. Habitual movements could include: the unique manner in which you squat when you line up a putt, the way you hold a club as you study and prepare for a shot, a gesture of a hand or arm as you approach the ball, taking a club out of the bag.

The only limitation on your choice of an anchor is that it be "clean"—not already associated with an experience on or off the golf course. For example, looking at a wedding ring would not be a good V-anchor because it's already connected to very powerful emotional experiences.

Making Anchors Work Automatically

To fully establish these anchors so they'll be useful later on, it's necessary to "fire" them consciously three or four times a day for a week or two until the anchored emotional state can be activated within a few seconds. Then forget about conscious anchoring, letting the process become part of your unconscious mind. The conscious act of firing an anchor consists of deliberately looking at the external visual cue, or listening to the external sound cue or moving in an habitual way, while associating the cue or movement with the actual emotional feeling of a resourceful state.

If you would like to *establish* the finger-pressing anchor related to the good shot which you identified as Sherlock, press your finger on the specific part of your body and consciously see the internal image and hear the internal sound that were part of the remembered shot. The finger pressure should be maintained until you feel the return of the full force of the emotional sensations you had while hitting that past shot. Repeat this process several times each day for the next week or two. With this anchor-firing practice you'll eventually be able to reactivate the emotional state associated with the past shot very quickly—in a matter of seconds.

If you want to contextualize the anchor for that past good shot, select either a habitual movement, an *external* visual cue, or an *external* auditory cue that is always present on the golf course to serve as a new substitute anchor. Practice firing this new anchor three or four times a day for several weeks until it works as well as the finger pressure; this may be done on or off the course. When off the course just think about the external cue or make the habitual movement until the emotional state can be produced in a few seconds.

One professional golfer looks at the printed logo on his golf bag; it's his V-anchor for generating determination. Another golfer looks at the end of the grip on his clubs; this is his V-anchor to activate a state of concentration. A third golfer listens to the rhythmic sound of his clubs rattling in the bag as he walks between shots; this A-anchor returns him to a feeling of calmness after he makes a poor shot.

Each of these golfers used finger pressure on some part of their body when they first identified and anchored their resource state during the Sherlock Holmes Exercise. They fired the finger-pressure anchor on the golf course to regenerate the desired state. Then they transferred the feeling anchored by the finger pressure to a new A-, V-, or K-anchor that is always present on the course.

The golfers practiced firing these new anchors both on and off the course. When at home or in the office, they imagined they were on the course. Then they saw, heard, or felt their particular anchor, and consciously generated their desired emotional state. After they were able to generate the desired state in association with a particular anchor within a matter of seconds, they stopped formal practice and allowed their unconscious minds to take over—just the way hearing a certain song can automatically generate a feeling of love for a special person.

ANCHORING

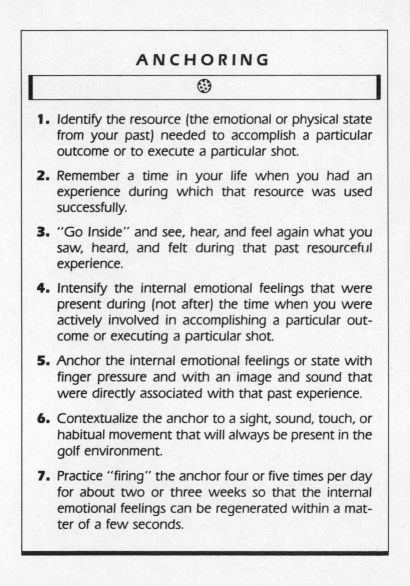

1. Identify the resource (the emotional or physical state from your past) needed to accomplish a particular outcome or to execute a particular shot.
2. Remember a time in your life when you had an experience during which that resource was used successfully.
3. "Go Inside" and see, hear, and feel again what you saw, heard, and felt during that past resourceful experience.
4. Intensify the internal emotional feelings that were present during (not after) the time when you were actively involved in accomplishing a particular outcome or executing a particular shot.
5. Anchor the internal emotional feelings or state with finger pressure and with an image and sound that were directly associated with that past experience.
6. Contextualize the anchor to a sight, sound, touch, or habitual movement that will always be present in the golf environment.
7. Practice "firing" the anchor four or five times per day for about two or three weeks so that the internal emotional feelings can be regenerated within a matter of a few seconds.

Now that you know how to anchor a resource, you'll learn the practical uses of anchors in subsequent chapters.

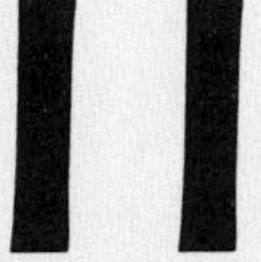

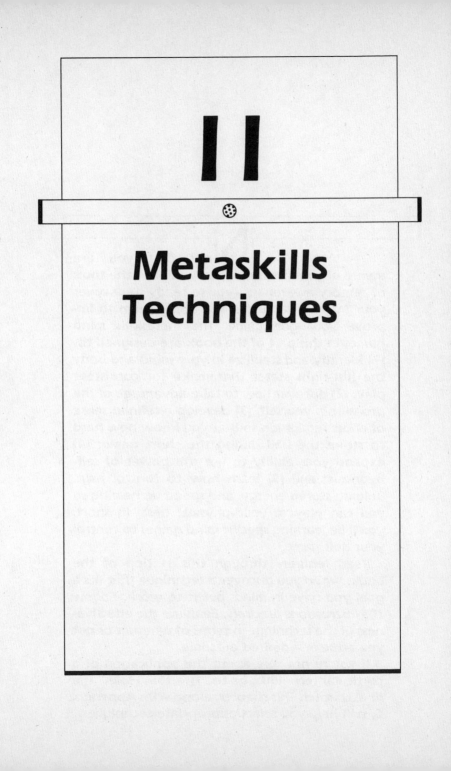

Metaskills Techniques

Now that you are aware of your mental-detective skills—the tools of sensory awareness—you're ready to uncover your internal resources and apply them to improve your golf game. The metaskills mind games in this part of the book are designed to: (1) identify and stabilize in your mind and body the just-right states that make for consistent play; (2) discover how to take advantage of the pro within yourself; (3) develop a refined sense of effort regulation so that you know how hard to strike the ball during the short game; (4) expand your ability to use the power of self-hypnosis; and (5) learn how to control pain, unleash stored energy, and speed up healing so you can play at your physical best. In short, you'll be learning specific mind games to control your golf game.

Read leisurely through this section of the book. When you discover a technique that fits a goal you have in mind, put it to work. *Follow the instructions precisely.* Evaluate the effectiveness of the technique in terms of whether or not you achieve a desired outcome.

If you're not sure about the application of a particular technique, go to "The 19th Hole," the final chapter. This chapter, along with Appendix C, will help you select appropriate techniques.

FOUR

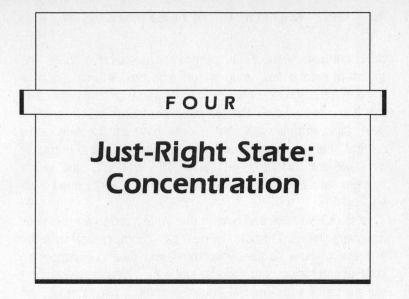

Just-Right State: Concentration

There's a 15th club in golf. You don't hit the ball with it, or even see it, for that matter. Call it mood, the emotional state you bring to the course, or to a shot, that determines how you use the other tools at your command. That mood can change as quick as lightning, depending on your values and how your mind works, consciously and unconsciously.

Some days you're hot. The ball flies so true, it's as though someone were standing far down the fairway with a large magnet in hand; frequently trees uproot themselves and step in front of the few badly struck shots, bumping the ball out of harm's way; the four-inches-in-diameter cup all of a sudden seems crater wide.

On other days it's hot of a different sort. You're hot under the collar. Glaciers hustle along faster than the gang ahead; somehow, blades of grass on the fairway turn into steel and redirect a solidly struck ball into a jungle jail. You don't know whether, as the country song goes, to shoot yourself or go bowling.

Mood swings are as important as the golf swing; and your

mind controls both. Fortunately, you don't have to be the victim of your not-so-good states; you can either maintain a good state or quickly change it from lousy to just right. You can learn to make all the between-shot time work to quiet your mind during each shot and to have all the necessary mental and physical resources readily and automatically available for making good shots. If you don't, golf might regress into Mark Twain's description of it as "a good walk spoiled."

In Part 1 you learned how to use your mind to access your inner resources. This and the next two chapters deal with the process of how to use your mind and inner resources to control and swing your moods, since they dramatically affect the swing of your club. If you're a scratch player, say, and take a quadruple bogey on the second hole, I have a way to keep that instant anger from making the remaining 16 holes almost as miserable. I'll teach you how to uncover and remain in touch with your feelings of confidence so that you can perform comfortably at the peak of your capacity when the chips are down. In essence, you'll learn how to get into the just-right states that are conducive to hitting all sorts of shots well, using the anchoring process described in the previous chapter.

A few golfers I know use a natural, unconscious process of anchoring just-right states. For example, David Graham unconsciously repeats to himself the rhyming phrase "Low and slow" as an auditory anchor to activate the proper form and mood to regulate taking away his club on tee shots. Whenever he approaches a tee in tournament play, Peter Jacobsen automatically looks at the gallery as a visual anchor, and in some way absorbs spectators' energy as a means to get more power into his tee shots. My wife, Edna, says to herself, "Let the clubhead fly," just before take-away as a way to generate the feeling of hitting the ball with zip at impact.

In each of the three cases David, Peter, and Edna "fire"

their anchors automatically, without conscious thought. They just find themselves doing it. And I'll bet that you have an anchor or two tucked away in your unconscious mind that work for you.

I have developed several step-by-step anchoring processes that you can use to get and keep yourself in the just-right state for hitting each shot facing you at the moment. These anchors evolved from my systematic study of what athletes in many different sports do to generate and stabilize their moods. I refer to them generally as just-right anchors.

All the just-right anchors have the same basic steps, but there are among them some slight differences in their development and application. The basic steps were presented in Chapter 3. In addition to direct recall of emotional states associated with past resourceful experiences, I also use music, color, and metaphorical images to access appropriate resources and to stabilize just-right states. As you study these metaskills techniques, you may find several of them more to your liking than others.

For convenience I've grouped these anchoring techniques into categories that represent the three underlying states referred to earlier—concentration, confidence, and mind-body unity. The present chapter focuses on concentration. The next two chapters deal with confidence and mind-body unity.

In the remainder of this chapter you will learn how to generate and maintain concentration. The next two chapters will focus on confidence first, and then on getting into the "zone."

Strange as it seems, the epitome of concentration is paying attention to absolutely nothing. Some golf pros accidentally stumble onto this when they talk about hitting "a no-brainer." For every golfer at every level, thinking about not thinking is close to impossible.

We'll start by whittling golf thoughts down to one per shot—it isn't so hard to achieve as it might seem. The one thought—what I call a *cue,* or a *swing key*—is the thing that helps trigger a rhythmic effort. The choice of the right cue is partly based, as you might have guessed, on the form of sensory information easiest for you to process—auditory, visual, or kinesthetic—while you're swinging. It's also based on what works.

In my own case, for example, when I pay sole attention to increasing clubhead speed at impact—a K-cue—my arms become tense and I hurry the swing, hitting from the top. I end up losing what I want: power and distance. However, if I concentrate on seeing the club hit the back of the ball—a V-cue—my swing is satisfactory and provides lots of power. Although these two cues are important for a good swing, only one is helpful to me. Only I could have discovered that, just as only you can sift out which cues are most useful for you.

Uptime Anchor

The Uptime Anchor is one metaskills technique that will help you identify the most useful cues for you. It is particularly useful for beginners and high handicappers. When you've identified them, you can decide which ones, when attended to solely, will elicit your most intensive level of concentration.

Brian was a middle-handicap (20) golfer seeking to improve his concentration. He was utterly confused by all the advice he'd gotten from pros and books. He couldn't distinguish what was important.

"Let's work on getting the ball to fly straight to a target with my 9-iron," he told me on the practice range.

"Hit a few balls and pay attention to what you become aware of *naturally* as you set up and swing," I said. "Set up, turn, swing, and hit without giving yourself directions, sort of mindlessly, and notice whatever you see, hear, or feel on the outside."

After Brian hit eight or so shots, I asked him what he *saw,* on the outside, that seemed useful. He mentioned his target, his hands and feet, the clubhead behind the ball, and the club-head moving back. These are all "cues" for Brian.

"Fine," I said, "and what did you *feel*?" Once again I wanted him to notice *external* sensations—on the skin and in his muscles and joints. I told him to scan his body for muscle tension in all the important parts of his swing such as the grip with his hands, the swing of his arms and wrist action on take-away, the shoulder turn, and leg and hip action during the weight shift.

Brian said he felt his fingers on the club, turning his shoulders, the wind in his face, the shaft on his shoulder after follow-through, and oh, yes, a small stone under his shoe.

"And what did you *hear*?"

"Hardly anything at all, except the truck in the background, the *whoosh* of my club a couple of times when I swung. Yeah, when I heard the truck, the shot wasn't very good."

I said I wanted him to swing while paying attention to only *one* of those sensory cues at a time. He first chose the shoulder turn, a K-cue. Before he hit the ball, I wondered what he thought would be an acceptable performance on a scale of one to ten.

"About an eight or a nine."

"You're too tough on yourself, like a lot of players," I said. "Hogan didn't always get tens, remember, and you're a twenty handicapper."

He settled on seven.

"Okay, go ahead and hit a few balls while paying strict attention to the muscles that control the turn of your shoulders. Nothing else. And concentrate on that shoulder turn throughout the *entire* process."

Brian hit about six or seven balls, all but two of which were at least seventh-heaven. Two were better than sevens and one, he felt, was as pure as he could strike a 9-iron. A solid-perfect ten.

"I can't believe I could hit the ball so well," he said, while admitting that he'd lost concentration on the two shots that went sideways.

"Let's anchor the feelings of making those good shots in relation to paying attention to the shoulder turn," I said. "Creating this uptime anchor is a process of associating one cue with the physical feelings involved in executing *the entire swing.* We'll use a visual anchor, a part of your body, or piece of equipment you'll always have with you."

Brian chose his class ring.

"Not a good idea," I said. "Your ring is associated with school. Not that school is bad, but it makes the ring 'dirty' for my purposes."

"How about looking at my left shoe? It's always visible."

"Fine, and this is how I want you to create the anchor. First, remember all the physical sensations of hitting those good 9-iron shots—the muscle tension and the mechanics involved in the swing as you were paying attention to your shoulder turn on the backswing."

Brian looked out ahead while swinging his club gently, nodded, and said he was getting it.

"Now, as you look at your left shoe, say to yourself, 'I'm storing in my shoe the feeling of hitting my 9-iron shots while paying attention to my shoulder turn.' Put those swing feelings into your left shoe."

"Whaaaaat?" Brian was not comfortable talking to a shoe.

"Humor me," I said. "Pretend you're storing all the muscle feelings and movements you used during those shots in your shoe." Brian peered at his shoe for about ten seconds, then said, "Okay, now what?"

I asked how he'd done it, how he'd stored his swing feelings in such an unfamiliar way.

"I put a small movie screen on top of my shoe and ran a movie of me making a good shot," he replied. "I saw the ball jump off the club and sail down the practice range."

"And the feelings? The swing mechanics? The shoulder turn? Did you store all of them too?"

"As I was watching my miniature movie screen, I was feeling the swing," he told me, "especially the shoulder turn."

I told Brian to choose another cue from his earlier swings, something he had *seen*. He chose the width of his stance, the distance between his feet, and concentrated on it while hitting another half-dozen shots.

Most of the shots were lousy. Fives at best. Not worth anchoring.

He picked another V-cue, watching the clubhead move back straight from the ball for the first twelve inches. This time his practice shots were up to his standard of excellence. I had him "stack" that cue into his left shoe.

We went on like this for quite a while, experimenting, picking cues he thought were important and then hitting shots with only one of them in his mind at a time. Some he rejected; some he anchored. I also told him to identify and anchor uptime cues for other specific situations—fairway woods, bunker shots, putting.

Near the end of the process Brian asked, "When and how do I fire this anchor?"

"The only time I want you to fire it," I replied, "is when you lose concentration while playing, when you find yourself thinking about too many things, and when you're not hitting the ball well. And the way to fire it is to merely look at your left shoe and say, 'Okay, unconscious mind, take over.'"

"How will that make me concentrate?"

"Concentration is paradoxical. The less you think about,

the more you concentrate. Honest. And the better you'll hit golf balls. You'll be as good as your body and swing allow. You just demonstrated this principle while you were building the anchor.

"You were able to hit fine shots while concentrating on only one cue. That meant your unconscious mind was attending to all the rest of the stuff that made the shot good. It was free to do that because your conscious mind was not interfering.

"You were in what a pro friend of mine, Bill Adams, calls a 'trusting state.' Firing the anchor puts you back into that state."

I told Brian to make sure he understood the difference between practice and playing. Practice was for concentrating on only one of his important cues at a time. Five minutes for shoulder turn, five minutes for clubhead moving back the first 12 inches behind the ball, and so on.

"When you're on the course," I said, "just play. Get into that trusting state and stay there."

The uptime anchor may not be for you if you're a low handicap golfer. It could be more distracting than helpful, for you're already skilled at not paying attention to swing details.

UPTIME ANCHOR

1. Select a part of your body or equipment that will serve as a "clean" V-anchor.

2. Identify the club and the particular shot you want to improve (putting, bunker shots, fairway woods).

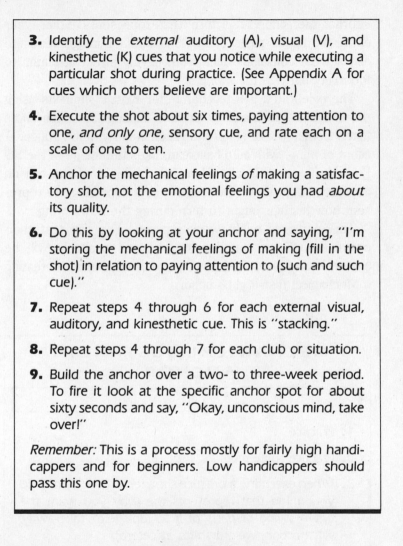

3. Identify the *external* auditory (A), visual (V), and kinesthetic (K) cues that you notice while executing a particular shot during practice. (See Appendix A for cues which others believe are important.)

4. Execute the shot about six times, paying attention to one, *and only one*, sensory cue, and rate each on a scale of one to ten.

5. Anchor the mechanical feelings *of* making a satisfactory shot, not the emotional feelings you had *about* its quality.

6. Do this by looking at your anchor and saying, "I'm storing the mechanical feelings of making (fill in the shot) in relation to paying attention to (such and such cue)."

7. Repeat steps 4 through 6 for each external visual, auditory, and kinesthetic cue. This is "stacking."

8. Repeat steps 4 through 7 for each club or situation.

9. Build the anchor over a two- to three-week period. To fire it look at the specific anchor spot for about sixty seconds and say, "Okay, unconscious mind, take over!"

Remember: This is a process mostly for fairly high handicappers and for beginners. Low handicappers should pass this one by.

Mechanical Just-Right Anchor

Another way to increase your concentration is by using a Mechanical Just-Right Anchor. It consists of making an internal metaphorical picture that represents either your entire swing or parts of it. This kind of image tends to distract the conscious mind from paying direct attention to too many parts of the swing.

The celebrated golf teacher Peter Kostis suggests using the image of touch-and-go airplane landings for pitch shots taken from a foot or so off the green in fairly heavy rough. A client of mine, with a 16 handicap, uses the image of the St. Louis arch as a visual anchor for the flight of the ball on approach shots. Peter Jacobsen sees a door hinge to represent how his hips ought to turn during the downswing.

These images might work for you. You can test their usefulness. Ones you develop yourself probably will be better. In any case, the following are instructions for creating a Mechanical Just-Right Anchor.

MECHANICAL JUST-RIGHT ANCHOR

1. Practice.
2. Practice some more.
3. When executing a practice shot, let an image pop into your mind that represents the way you want the entire swing or parts of it to look (e.g., take-away, wrist action, weight shifts, et cetera).
4. Hit several balls to determine if the shot stays fine with that spontaneous image.

5. Reinforce that V-anchor by hitting three or four of those particular shots several times a week for a week or two.

6. Reinforce the V-anchor, off the course, several times a day for about a week. Visualize door hinges, airplanes, or whatever, at home or the office. If anyone should inquire about the smile on your face, hand him this book.

7. After completing step 6, let your unconscious mind take over. Do nothing more.

FIVE

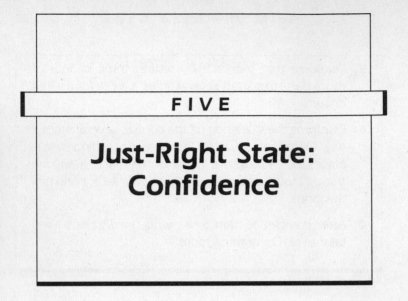

Just-Right State: Confidence

A common desired outcome for all golfers is to have confidence that they can execute the shot facing them at the moment. It's the same as the common desire for all humans to catch the next available whiff of air. Confidence in golf is a bit tougher than breathing—it comes with experience.

To build their confidence many golfers say to themselves, "I've played well in the past, so I can play well today." However, merely saying that is not enough to establish a lasting state of confidence. Generalizations about past performance don't work. What's needed to become confident is automatic and repeated generation of *specific* memories of hitting good shots. Here is one metaskills technique you can use to produce a genuine feeling of confidence.

Golf-Shot Resource Anchor

I helped one PGA Tour golfer build his confidence and access the just-right states for hitting several kinds of specific shots by using an anchoring technique that involved "stacking." An anchor is stacked when you associate more than one idea or feeling with it.

Randy, my touring pro, wanted to make his tee shots more consistent. Tee shots that flew all over the place eroded his confidence. Randy had already determined that one of his mechanical "keys" for driving was putting pressure on the club with the last three fingers of his left hand. To remind himself to have a firm grip at impact, he would deliberately and *routinely* squeeze those fingers *during his preparation* for all tee shots. The squeeze became his anchor for drives.

As we stood on the first tee, I told him to examine what the shot demanded and to remember a past successful drive he'd made on a similar hole. Because he'd played so often all over the country, that wasn't difficult.

Randy took his normal pose, looking down the fairway from behind the ball, holding his driver in his left hand.

"Now, I want you to *be very precise about remembering* and anchoring that similar shot," I said. "See, hear, and feel what you saw, heard, and felt then, until you become aware of the emotional state you were in *while* you were actually addressing and hitting the ball, not the feelings after you hit it." How he felt *after* a successful shot is obvious—and useless.

It took Randy a while, but he said, "I've got it. I was really eager to hit the ball. I couldn't wait to give it a ride."

"How do you know you felt eager?" I asked. "What sensations in your body let you know you felt eager? Really pay attention to sensations that indicated eagerness—in your shoulders, chest, stomach, arms, wherever."

"My forearms really felt alive, tingly," he said. "I get that feeling a lot when I want to crush one."

"Before anchoring that feeling," I said, "let's do a prior test of its usefulness. Generate that feeling strongly right now, and in your mind hit a ball from this tee. As you make that shot mentally, find out if it turns out the way you want it to."

I told him that if his mental shot wasn't up to his required level of performance, he was to select another prior shot, identify the emotional state associated with it, and test it before anchoring. He said his mental shot turned out just fine.

So I said, "Anchor that feeling of aliveness in your forearms by squeezing your last three fingers on the club. Match the amount of finger squeeze with the amount of aliveness you feel in your forearms as you relive that previous good shot."

I told him to *prepare for this present shot as he normally would,* and to generate that feeling of eagerness by squeezing his fingers and then releasing the squeeze as soon as he felt eager. I emphasized that he proceed to address the ball as he always had, applying no more or less pressure on the club than normal, and then hit the ball *without any thought whatsoever.* Just hit it.

The shot bore off on a long fade trajectory, landing on the right side of the fairway. After the ball came to rest I had Randy evaluate the quality of the shot again to make sure the emotional state from the prior shot was just right.

Randy said, "That's exactly the shot I had in mind. I had that same feeling of eagerness too. That's neat."

We repeated the process for several other tee shots on different holes, each time "stacking" other emotional feelings associated with past tee shots into the same K-anchor—squeezing the last three fingers of the left hand on the club.

In essence Randy created a *contextualized anchor*—a *physical movement that he naturally uses every time* he prepares to make a tee shot. After he established the anchor with repeated practice during the following weeks, it fired automatically because it was a part of his normal preparatory routine.

I repeated the entire anchoring process with him for fairway shots, for pitch-and-run shots, for bunker shots, and for several different kinds of putts. He created a *new K-anchor for each kind of shot:* a weight-shift onto his left leg for pitch shots, placement of his left hand on top of the grip as he squatted to survey the intended line of putts, and a knee bend for bunker shots. Most of them were positions or movements that Randy normally used as "keys" *during his preparation* for each kind of shot, and into which he stored or mentally associated emotions which he had recalled from previous shots in similar circumstances.

Then I asked him what he had learned from the process.

"I could recall past shots quite fast, once I got the hang of it," he said. "And I found I wasn't brooding over shots the way I used to. I was too busy thinking of the shot at hand."

Randy had one question: Was he supposed to do this anchoring process every time he played a round of golf? If so, he worried that there wouldn't be time for pleasant chitchat. In this kind of deal Randy doesn't like to be a silent partner.

I told him to *stack the anchors* only for a few rounds, anchoring feelings associated *with about ten good shots in each anchor*. By that time he will have stacked enough feelings of confidence to make all sorts of shots. And the anchors would fire automatically.

"I only fire the anchor consciously if I lack confidence?" he asked.

"Right."

"And if I'm faced with a shot I'm not sure about, can I go through what we did today?"

"Yes, but *only during practice rounds*. Don't use this

process in tournament play. I want you to direct your mind to playing each shot, one at a time. And fire the anchor only if you think it's absolutely necessary to change your state."

The following is an outline of the steps involved in creating your own just-right anchors for various golf shots. Essentially, you'll be anchoring confidence in many specific forms, over and over.

GOLF-SHOT RESOURCE ANCHOR

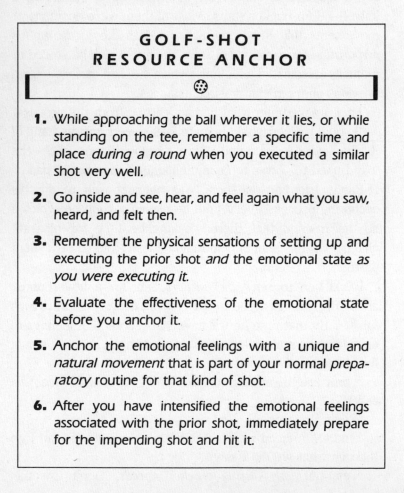

1. While approaching the ball wherever it lies, or while standing on the tee, remember a specific time and place *during a round* when you executed a similar shot very well.
2. Go inside and see, hear, and feel again what you saw, heard, and felt then.
3. Remember the physical sensations of setting up and executing the prior shot *and* the emotional state *as you were executing it.*
4. Evaluate the effectiveness of the emotional state before you anchor it.
5. Anchor the emotional feelings with a unique and *natural movement* that is part of your normal *preparatory* routine for that kind of shot.
6. After you have intensified the emotional feelings associated with the prior shot, immediately prepare for the impending shot and hit it.

7. Stack the emotional feelings of about ten different successful shots in the same anchor.
8. Practice "firing" the anchor three or four times a day for a week or so—at home, in the office, on the course, wherever. By then you should be playing on automatic pilot.

If occasionally you lack confidence in a particular shot, you can consciously fire the appropriate anchor before going through your preshot routine. An especially difficult shot or a string of bad holes might call for this sort of thing. It's always better to fire your anchor instead of your caddy, or your clubs. However, *in tournament play, don't go through this process, or any other metaskills techniques* for that matter. They're meant for practice, to tune your unconscious mind to operate automatically.

The length of time Randy and I spent building his golf-shot resource anchors was extensive. He had the luxury of belonging to a club and had lots of time to practice. So what about public-course players squeezed between a slow foursome and an anxious posse of swift shooters behind? Most courses are already plagued by slow play; more excuses for delay simply won't be tolerated.

That's one reason why I've emphasized the abundance of time that exists between shots. Those cumulative minutes average out to about thirteen a hole. Use the time getting to the ball, on foot or in a cart, to develop this anchoring process.

You've already assimilated lots of useful information from watching the previous shot come to rest. From 150-plus yards, for instance, you know whether the ball is in the fairway or rough, and whether the next shot will be with a wood, long iron, or more lofted club. With this in mind, even before you've put the club back in the bag and moved a step forward, you can be thinking about a previous shot similar to the one you'll be facing. Like Randy you'll be surprised at how quickly one will surface. Most golfers play on a "home" course, public or private, which makes recall even easier.

Competitive-State Anchor

Teeing off on the first tee is frequently an anxious moment for many golfers, amateur and professional. Often the anxiety is a manifestation of a lack of confidence, if only for the moment. As most golfers know, when we lose confidence, our golf swing often goes kerflooey. However, if the first hole is played well, we get confident again, and usually the rest of the round goes well. What's necessary is the ability to be competition-keen and stay that way. An anchor can do that.

A competitive-state anchor can be created by playing in your mind a complete and successful round of golf (on the tournament course) the day or night before a tournament, paying attention to the positive feelings generated during the fantasy round. These positive feelings of the fantasy round can be anchored in a common, ordinary movement, like stroking your chin, folding your hands, interlacing your fingers, pulling an ear, scratching your head, or making a fist.

The idea is to play each hole mentally with successful shots, stacking the feelings of accomplishment and confidence in *one anchor* as you go along. If, in your mind, a shot doesn't turn out right, replay it several times until it does. If a particular shot continues to be a bad one in your fantasy, never mind. Go ahead to where it lies and make a good shot, anchoring that good feeling. Later on you can devote practice time to correcting the errant fantasy shot.

When finished, you will have anchored (stacked) good feelings of confidence 72 times, more or less, and you will have mentally reviewed the course in advance of the tournament. Practice firing this anchor several times a day until it generates confidence in a matter of seconds.

When you arrive at the golf course on the day or days of the tournament, and as you approach the first tee, fire the competitive-state anchor. If you become overly anxious while playing, fire the competitive-state anchor again to swing you back to a better frame of mind.

COMPETITIVE-STATE ANCHOR

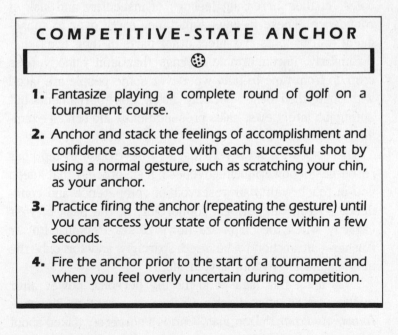

1. Fantasize playing a complete round of golf on a tournament course.
2. Anchor and stack the feelings of accomplishment and confidence associated with each successful shot by using a normal gesture, such as scratching your chin, as your anchor.
3. Practice firing the anchor (repeating the gesture) until you can access your state of confidence within a few seconds.
4. Fire the anchor prior to the start of a tournament and when you feel overly uncertain during competition.

Personal Power

Playing a successful fantasy round of golf before a tournament and anchoring feelings of confidence may not overcome more pervasive feelings of insecurity. Sometimes anxiety starts hours or perhaps days before a tournament begins, manifested in stomach discomfort and headaches. Sometimes insecurity begins to gnaw at a player's mind toward the end of a tournament when he or she is on top of the leader board. For those who haven't developed ways to cope with their fears, bogeys and double bogeys often crop up on the last few holes, further increasing feelings of insecurity and lack of confidence. These feelings sometimes carry over to subsequent tournaments and infect other parts of their lives.

Similarly, uncomfortable feelings that limit effectiveness crop up from time to time whenever some people are faced with doing their best—not only during golf tournaments but during job interviews, sales presentations, and school examinations as well.

There's a way, however, that I've developed to tap your resources of powerful effectiveness; it's a process that keeps you in touch with your reservoir of competence and confidence so you can perform comfortably at the peak of your capacity when the chips are down. It's a Personal Power Anchor—an anchor to be used sparingly and for only the most significant events in your life.

I hit upon this idea of anchoring personal power after thinking about what Carlos Castaneda wrote in his book *Journey to Ixtlan.** Don Juan, Carlos's sorcerer, talked about the importance of being prepared to face fear and death

*Published by Simon and Schuster (New York, 1972), pp. 181–189.

gracefully and courageously. He said that each person should identify a personal place of power—an actual geographical place where he has experienced a sense of awe combined with exhilaration, strength, and confidence.

Whenever that person reaches a goal of utmost significance, he is to return to his place of power, either in actuality or in fantasy, and "deposit" the feelings of powerful effectiveness there. Then, according to Don Juan, when death approaches over his left shoulder, he is to return to his place of power, either in actuality or in fantasy, gather the deposited power into his being, and dance the dance of death—that is, face death courageously, replacing the feelings of fear with power.

Don Juan created a process to deal with death; I have converted it to deal with living. My process, the Personal Power Anchor, consists of identifying your place of power, "storing" the feelings associated with your own experiences of competence, and eventually tapping those resources of power when you're faced with events of utmost significance in your life that are sometimes frightening or anxiety provoking. Essentially, the process is an anchor that you fire to empower yourself to make living full of rich experiences instead of anxious ones. Here's how it works.

Identify a Personal Place of Power. In your mind go back to a specific time and place—a place that overwhelmed you by its beauty, where you were at one with nature and the universe, where you experienced a sense of excitement and confidence. That place may be close by or hundreds of miles away. It could be in the mountains, near a lake or the ocean, in the midst of a forest or a field of grass, under a majestic tree, next to a cool stream, in the rain or snow—no matter—just a very special place for you.

Go inside and see, hear, and feel what you saw, heard, and felt when you were in that place. Notice the light, shadows, and colors; listen to the pitch, volume, and tone of the sounds; and especially feel the sensations of awe, excitement, and confidence that you felt while in that special place. That special place is going to be where you, in your imagination, can "store" all the feelings you've had when you did things superbly, powerfully, and independently. It's also a place where you can eventually store all of the feelings of power that you'll experience in the future.

Identify Past Experiences of Power. Remember and relive a time in your life when you performed a task, any task, superbly. Perhaps you felt a sense of graceful and easy power as you played your very best competitive round of golf. You might have felt extremely satisfied after giving a fine speech before a large audience. You might have been excited after completing a top-notch interview. You might have been really pleased after playing a part in a school or college play. Or you might have had a deep feeling of caring and love after writing a letter to a special person.

Relive that past experience of powerful effectiveness. See, hear, and feel again what you saw, heard, and felt then. See the things you saw on the inside—in your mind—and on the outside. Pay close attention to the submodalities; *most of all,* feel those physical sensations of powerful effectiveness and confidence.

Anchor the Powerful Experience with a K-anchor—something that is natural and unobtrusive, such as touching your face or making a fist. Associate the K-anchor with a special image and sound which are directly related to the past experience.

Create a Storehouse of Power. Fire the K-anchor and when the feelings of power are strong, "deposit" those feelings in the one particular spot you have chosen as your personal place of power. In your mind, metaphorically see that power stored there.

Increase the amount of stored power by repeating the same process with other past experiences of achievement and with similar experiences you'll have in the future. "Stack" feelings of power from each new experience into the *same* K-anchor.

Tap the Storehouse of Power. When you want to perform superbly in crucial situations—when the chips are down—you can recapture the feelings of powerful effectiveness. Fire the K-anchor, go to your place of power in actuality or in fantasy, and see the imaginary storehouse of power. Do this several hours or the night before you want to perform at your very best. Remove as *little* power as necessary by metaphorically grasping a small portion of it in your hands. Actually reach out, "grasp" power, and then bring your hands to your chest until you feel confidently energized.

PERSONAL POWER ANCHOR

1. Identify your geographical place of power.
2. Identify a past experience when you performed at your very best.
3. Anchor the physical sensations of effectiveness and power with a natural, unobtrusive gesture (K-anchor), a special image, and a special sound or word.
4. Go to your place of power, in actuality or in fantasy; fire the K-anchor and metaphorically "deposit" the feelings of power in that place.

5. For each past and future experience of power repeat Steps 2 through 4 and stack the feelings of power associated with them in the same K-anchor.

6. To tap your storehouse of power when faced with a very important task, fire the common K-anchor, go to your place of power in actuality or in fantasy, and see the storehouse of power that you deposited there. Do this the night before or several hours before you want to perform at your very best.

7. Take as *little* power as necessary and bring it into your body until you feel confidently energized.

SIX

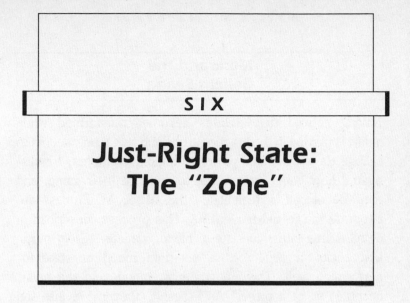

Just-Right State: The "Zone"

After making a tee shot right down the middle or after an approach that lands within a foot or two of the pin, golfers often say, "If only I could bottle it!" As a matter of fact, the golf swing that produces those shots is bottled in the nervous system.

When a golfer is in the right state of mind, he can execute that bottled swing throughout an entire round. When this occurs, mind, mood, and movement are solidly melded. A sense of harmony in the golfer's body produces a rhythmical and effortless swing; his attention is riveted on each shot, yet there is no conscious concentration; his confidence is unwavering. He feels as if he's in another world or in a trance—the state of being in the "zone."

This chapter focuses on the use of music, color, and images to uncork the bottled swing.

Music and the Golfer's Swing

Having noticed that athletes become transformed when music is playing in the practice arena and that music seems to change the rhythm and power of their movements, I investigated how golfers use music to enhance their game, and then developed a technique—the M & M Process—to integrate music and movement. This process, described in detail a little later, consists of having athletes select music that elicits or reinforces a just-right mood or state for performing well. Their movements, mood, and the music become "all of a piece." As a result, they move into the "zone" and play more consistently.

Since the golf swing is rhythmical, and since most golfers have a comfortable tempo for playing an entire round, it makes sense to use music to create a just-right state for both. Let's see how some golfers have used music to enhance their game.

The Use of Music to Maintain Swing Tempo

A former client of mine uses music to correct a tendency to play too fast after a few bad shots or when he feels rushed by a foursome behind. When he rushes his shots, he bypasses his normal preshot preparatory pattern. Consequently, his arms and legs become tense and the coordinated movement of his swing becomes quick and jerky. Naturally, his shots turn out to be less than what he is capable of hitting.

To correct this, he identified several different songs that reflect his preferred playing pace and swing tempo. Whenever he had a bad shot during practice, or whenever his normal playing pace was interrupted, he deliberately played one of his favorite songs. He listened to those songs while wearing a Walkman during practice rounds to get them anchored. The songs slowed him down and smoothed out his swing. Now, when playing in a tournament, the music automatically plays in his mind when trouble occurs.

Using Music to Quiet the Mind

Many golfers have developed the bad habit of giving themselves silent verbal instructions when they set up to the ball and as they're swinging. These instructions are okay *before* setting up to the ball, but there's nothing more disruptive to the mental regulation of the complex golf swing than internal talk *during* the setup and swing. You don't talk while anyone else is swinging; so be quiet on your own swing. Listening to music is a marvelous way to stop your internal voices so that your unconscious mind can assume control of your swing.

Ann Dickimson, a middle-handicapper, had difficulty with her tee shots because a constant flow of internal negative chatter bothered her. Don't slice, stay out of the trees—that sort of nonsense. Naturally, she even arrived at the first tee in a state of high anxiety.

She quickly corrected her mental state on the tee by humming to herself a phrase from Beethoven's Fifth Symphony. The music put her in a good mood and eliminated all internal talk during her setup and swing. Her tee shots became long and straight. She regained confidence and her anxiety stopped.

On a slightly different note, a number of golfers use music to regulate their pace for walking between shots and for preshot mental preparation. PGA touring pro Fuzzy Zoeller whistles while he's looking over a shot. Mike Sparks, a PGA pro at Ridgewood Country Club, sings "The Battle of New Orleans" when he's playing well.

A friend of mine primes himself to swing the club smoothly and approaches the game in a playful mood when he hears, in his mind, the Benny Goodman band playing "Sing, Sing, Sing." He changes the words of the song to "Swing, Swing, Swing." What could be more appropriate for golf?

The M & M Process

The M & M Process is a systematic way of using music to regulate your golf swing. It consists of matching specific elements of music with your entire swing or with specific parts of it. Here's how to do it.

Sitting in an armchair at home, see again in your mind a fine golf shot, paying close attention to the feel of the rhythm and power of the swing that produced the shot. Then listen to different kinds of pleasing music that you think will match the swing. Test the match between music and your imagined swing. If the images of the remembered shot are clear and positive, and if you can feel your muscles contract in harmony with the music, you've got a just-right match. Then it's time to take it out, first to the practice tee and then on the course for test runs.

On the practice tee hit several balls while listening to the selected music, using a Walkman or simply hearing it in your head. When you're satisfied that the music positively influences the tempo and effectiveness of your swing, anchor the music to your swing. While hearing the music in your mind, hit balls on the course or practice tee daily, or swing a club at home if you can't get to the range. Continue this practice for several weeks until the music becomes firmly associated with your swing. Eventually you'll discover that the music will automatically play in your head when you swing a club.

When developing your musical anchor on the golf course, it may be important for you to complete your normal preshot routine before you start the music in your mind. That is, decide how and where you will hit the ball and get into the address position first. If you start the music too soon, you may disrupt your swing altogether because you're not mentally prepared for the shot at hand.

Swing Elements. A more sophisticated application of music consists of matching specific elements of music with specific parts of your golf swing. The elements of music consist of its rhythm, or beat, its intensity, or "energy," its volume, and the personal meaning of the words, if any. The parts of your golf swing that could be matched with the music include: grip strength, waggle, pace and length of the backswing, speed of the club head at impact, and the follow-through.

For example, the rhythm of an entire piece of music, or even one musical phrase, might parallel your entire swing; a syncopated rhythm might be just right to emphasize the hand action at the bottom of the swing; a pause or extended note could regulate the amount of hesitation you want at the top of your backswing. The energy or loudness of a song might be appropriate for regulating the amount of effort needed to blast out of a buried lie in a sand trap, while quite the opposite level of musical energy would be more suitable for stroking a delicate downhill putt with a double break. A soft love ballad might be just right for a smooth approach shot, while a John Philip Sousa march could be more fitting for a long drive into the wind. The possibilities for "matches" between music and the golf swing are infinite.

Here are the steps to follow while using the M & M Process.

M & M PROCESS

1. Sitting somewhere comfortable at home, recall making a fine golf shot; or relive a shot you just made on the practice tee. See and hear what you saw and heard then, and feel again the rhythm and effort of your swing.
2. Identify several pieces of music you enjoy which you think might have the intensity, beat, rhythm, and harmony that match the entire swing or an element of it.
3. Test the match between the music and your swing. If the images of the remembered shot are clear and positive, if you can feel your muscles contract and relax in harmony with the music, then it's time for on-course encores.
4. Strap a Walkman to your waist and listen to the music while executing that preselected shot. If you don't have a Walkman, start the music in your mind.
5. If the shots are good, fire the musical anchor at home and on the practice range for two or three weeks, or until the music plays automatically in your head whenever you're about to make the shot on a golf course.
6. Evaluate the effectiveness of the process. If the quality of the shot decreases, change the music.

Follow the same steps to identify and anchor music that matches the just-right walking pace between shots. It is especially important to use a Walkman during practice rounds on the course so that you have the actual tempo of the music in mind and not what you thought the tempo should be.

Piece-of-Cake Anchor

Because of the capacity of music to affect one's emotional state intensely, I developed a special technique that capitalizes on integrating music, emotions related to a meaningful past experience, and shots that are particularly tough. These situations usually include: bunker shots; short downhill, breaking putts on a slick green; delicate chip shots from deep grass to a close-cut pin; or any other shot that bugs you. I call it the Piece-of-Cake Anchor because it's designed to transform your tough shots into easy ones that are consistently good.

A client, Nel Whiting, had a long-standing problem with bunker shots. She had the skill to make them; she had a 14 handicap and was club champion in her flight several times. She chunked sand shots too often, though, to the point of being "terrified" whenever she saw sand. Now her sand shots are a piece of cake. This is what we did together.

I tossed a ball into the middle of a big sand trap and said, "Does this shot remind you of a shot you've made somewhere else?"

After thinking for a moment she remembered one something like it at the Mid Ocean course in Bermuda.

I told her to prepare to make the sand shot, pretending she was at Mid Ocean, and step in and hit it out. She swung like a dishrag; the ball moved about a foot or two.

Earlier we had talked together, and she had said that whenever she's in a trap, she always hears a voice inside saying, "Follow through, now." And the voice really bugs her, causing her to put a death grip on the club and become tense in her chest.

Knowing this I asked, "What was going on inside of you on that last shot?"

"The same old voice, 'Follow through, now,'" she replied.

"How about the grip and tension?" I asked. "Were they present too?"

"Absolutely, as tight as ever," she answered.

At this point I asked her to find a piece of music that she really likes—one that she could put the words of her internal voice to. I knew she couldn't get rid of that voice. It had been with her for years. So I decided to have her use it constructively.

I wanted her to find a song that got her in the right state that would match the way she wanted to feel while hitting sand shots well—not just any old song, but one that had some meaning, one that reminded her of an experience unrelated to golf.

It didn't take her more than five seconds to come up with "San Francisco." I could tell by the smile and flush on her face that it did have meaning.

I tossed another ball into the trap and instructed her to go through her normal preshot routine, and *then* sing the words "Follow through, now," to the tune "San Francisco," while she was addressing the ball and swinging.

She swung and put the ball into the cup about forty feet away.

"Wow," I said, as Nel, her pro, and I watched with amazement. "Let's see if it'll work again." I tossed several more balls into the trap.

Nel took a few more shots, some good, some bad; she got all but one of them out of the trap. She realized that she was raising her head on some of the poorer shots, so I had her integrate another phrase about keeping her head down into the tune she was singing.

I queried her about the death grip and the tension in her chest; she said her grip was soft and she felt very relaxed during the entire shot.

Subsequently, Nel told me that she practiced the routine of associating the song with making sand shots for about an hour or so after we worked together, and regularly sang her song to herself when she had a sand shot to play during matches. I had her anchor the entire process to the act of grasping her sand wedge as she took it out of the bag.

In a letter a month or so after we had worked together, Nel wrote, "On the very first hole [of competition] my ball went into the bunker. No problem—I just sang my song and out onto the green went my dimpled ball—Success. The same success has come many times since. It's a wonderful feeling knowing I can make any bunker shot."

PIECE-OF-CAKE ANCHOR

1. Go to the practice tee, bunker, or putting green and practice a shot that you want to become more consistent.
2. When you pull it off, identify the emotional feeling associated with it (e.g., eagerness, patience, determination, gentleness).
3. Remember a song that holds a lot of meaning—one which pertains to a past experience unrelated to golf.

4. Relive that experience fully as you sing the song, so that the emotional feelings become more pronounced.
5. Go through your preshot routine and *then* sing the song silently in your head.
6. Hit the shot again and hear the song as you're setting up and swinging.
7. If the shots remain lousy, repeat steps two through six until a just-right emotion is identified.
8. When the emotion fits, anchor the song and the emotion with a K-anchor—a natural, habitual movement that you make during your preshot routine.
9. Reinforce the anchor until you can generate the same emotional state in a matter of a few seconds. (See Chapter 3).

A word of caution: If you use an emotional experience associated with a close friend or loved one, and if that relationship sours, discard that anchor (the song) and create a new one.

TIME DISTORTION

Swing tempo is usually a reflection of your inner pace. If you've been racing about town, chances are your swing will be fast when you get to the course. What's needed is a modification of your perception of time, inner and outer, to change the speed of your swing.

While working with some figure skaters in Sun Valley several years ago, I stumbled onto two very simple techniques that affect the timing of coordinated movement, like spinning in figure skating, twisting in diving, and swinging a golf club.

One of these metaskills techniques, the Counting Process, may remind you of the childhood game of hide-and-seek. You remember. When you were "it," you had to hide your eyes and count to one hundred, or some other high number. It seemed to take forever. The other, the Off-Ramp Technique, relates to the dramatic change in the sensation of speed when you leave a high-speed highway on the off ramp; then time and speed seem to slow down. One or both of these techniques will probably be useful if you want to slow down your backswing or speed up the movement of the clubhead through the impact area.

The Counting Process

This metaskills technique merely involves counting, *first very slowly, then as fast as possible.* Count silently to *ten* as slowly as possible. Then silently count to *ten* as quickly as possible; to *twenty* as quickly as possible, to *forty* as quickly as possible, and finally to *fifty* as fast as you can. Don't skip any number the way you might have when you played hide-and-seek. After you've finished the counting tasks, immediately hit a golf ball, paying attention to the tempo of your swing. The result will probably be the exact tempo you want because your perception of the time has been altered.

The Off-Ramp Technique

This technique consists of mentally traveling in an automobile on a superhighway at maximum speed while watching rapidly passing center-line markings, and seeing the light poles and trees peripherally on the side of the road. Listen to the hum of the engine and the *whoosh* of the wind as your car speeds along. Feel the vibration of the wheels through the chassis against your feet and the movement of the steering wheel in your hands. Now imagine it's time to leave the highway as the exit ramp suddenly appears a very short distance ahead. Apply the brakes, hear the tires squeal, and feel your body being thrust forward as you quickly slow down to thirty-five, twenty-five, and fifteen miles per hour in a matter of seconds. At this point the car will seem to be crawling along to the end of the ramp. When this mental process is complete, immediately hit a golf ball. The result will be a correction in the timing of your swing, either a slower backswing or a faster action in the impact area of your swing, depending upon what you're working on at the moment.

Color and the Golfer's Swing

You may remember the fellow I introduced at the beginning of the book, Ted Jackson, the eighty-two-year-old who wanted to hit better pitch shots from about ninety yards. As you did, Ted went through the Sherlock Holmes Exercise to rediscover a fine pitch he once hit at the Saxon Woods course in Scarsdale, New York. As you're about to, Ted discovered a colored-image anchor, in which seeing one bird gets him closer to bagging another.

When he had finished the Sherlock Holmes Exercise, during which he he recalled hitting a particularly fine pitch shot, I said, "Reproduce that swing here on the practice tee, but stay with that dream shot in your mind." He did.

After he had taken several practice swings, I placed a ball in front of him and said, "I want you to hit just short of the hundred-yard marker. But before you take the club away, go back in your mind to when you hit the shot so beautifully. Then swing and hit this ball as if you were actually there."

Once more Ted swung his mind years back to the fifth hole at Saxon Woods. Then he swung his club. "Wow, that's it," he said. "That's the way it was—and the way I want it."

"Repeat what you just did," I told him. "Only, this time, as you strike the ball, still pretending you're back at the scene of the earlier shot, let the ball change into a color, any color at all."

When Ted struck the ball again, he said, "Red! That's exactly what I want."

I asked him to do it once more and placed another ball in front of him. "Go back to Saxon Woods and relive that fifth-hole shot again. When you're fully back there, hit another ball and let the red color spontaneously become an image, any image at all."

After hitting the ball Ted laughed and said, "A flying red goose. That's what I see." The shot was identical to the first two. He was surprised and delighted.

"In the future," I said, "just think about the flying red goose when you're about to make approach shots, and let your unconscious mind do the rest."

COLORED-IMAGE ANCHOR

1. As you hit a shot well on the practice tee, let a color flash into your mind as the clubhead strikes the ball.
2. Repeat the shot and see the color again. If it was well hit, hit another ball and let the color change spontaneously into an image as the clubhead meets the ball.

3. Hit the same shot several more times while seeing the colored image in your mind as you watch the ball. Think of nothing else.
4. Anchor this colored image a few more times daily for two or three weeks until you see the colored image without conscious effort. (See Chapter 3).
5. If the shots are unsatisfactory, generate another colored image.

It's possible that color, like music, can be a distraction. But give it a full chance. Make sure you see the color at the moment of impact, not before.

Free-Swing Anchor

Anchored images need not be in color like Ted's goose. Any image can represent the feeling you want when you swing, and it can be generated out of any past experience.

According to most professional golfers the most effective swing is one that feels free and effortless. Consequently, if you can create a single image that represents the idea of freedom combined with effortlessness, you will create the right amount of freedom in your mind and body to make those effortless shots that feel so great. All you need to do is to remember a time in your life, *unrelated to golf,* when you really felt free. It might be a time when you were sunbathing on a beach, floating on a raft at the shore, or leaving school on graduation day.

While on the practice tee go back to that experience in

your mind to feel again the bodily sensations of freedom. When you have that feeling of freedom, remember a specific scene from that time that best represents the freedom you want when you swing.

Now set up to a ball and project an image of that scene onto the top of your hands as you are holding the club. When the image is clear and you feel free in your body, turn, swing, and hit the ball, keeping in mind that image projected onto your hands throughout the swing. How good was the shot? How did the swing feel? If it was good and felt effortless, you now have a new V-anchor, an image representing freedom.

Reinforce the new anchor whenever you practice, for several weeks, using all the clubs in your bag. When you can consistently generate effortless swings, forget about consciously projecting the image onto your hands. If your body ever gets taut when you swing, consciously fire the anchor again.

"Swish"

There's a process you can use to regain your composure after, say, a dubbed 6-iron from the middle of the fairway went splish-splash and cost you a career nine. It's called "Swish" and was invented by Richard Bandler, one of the founders of NLP. The name is apt, because when it works, and that's most of the time, it works quickly—*swish.* Its purpose is to bring about a lasting change in behavior or mood, exactly what's needed to be consistent on the golf course.

A few years ago I was working with one of my clients, Billy Musto, an aspiring professional who wanted to make the Pro Tour. He was becoming increasingly angry, banging his clubs against the ground, muttering to himself, and was about to give up. He had just mis-hit an easy approach shot to the 8th green. This followed a scrambling bogey on the 7th hole.

"Let's pack it in, Mac," he said angrily.

"That's certainly one choice," I replied. "But before we do that, let's do a 'swish' on your anger."

"A what?" he asked.

"Swish," I repeated. "It's a quick way to change your state. Here's what I want you to do. As you think about your anger, what color do you think would match it?"

"Red, deep red," he answered quickly.

"Okay," I said, holding the palm of my hand in front of his face. "Project an image of that deep red color here on my hand. Think about what you were doing that got you angry and at the same time make the palm of my hand bright red. Now really feel your anger."

Then I asked him what color reminded him of being calm and in control of his golf game and his general behavior. He said that blue was a good color for calmness.

"Now, Billy, remember a specific time when you were calm on the golf course, playing the way you're capable of playing, and see the color blue in your mind's eye." I paused a moment while he did that and asked, "What does it feel like?"

Billy's facial muscles softened a bit and he said, "I don't feel as angry."

"Fine," I said. "Keep seeing a blue color and that specific time when you were calm and relaxed."

Billy slowly appeared to relax as he stared into space, looking at the color blue in his mind.

"All right," I said, "now we're ready to swish. This is what I want you to do. See the palm of my hand deep red and at the same time see a small patch of blue, about the size of a dime, superimposed on the red in the lower left-hand corner of my hand."

I knew Billy was following my instructions because his

eyes moved up and down and his pupils contracted and dilated. He nodded and said curtly, "Now what?"

"Great," I replied, "apparently you're still angry."

He looked at me with the corners of his mouth turned down and nodded.

Continuing, I said, "What I want you to do is to *quickly* make the blue color expand and completely replace the red color on the palm of my hand. Do it as fast as you can when I say, 'Swish.' Ready . . . Swish!"

Billy's eyes defocused completely as he changed colors. Then I asked, "What's it feel like inside when you 'swish'?"

"I feel lighter and much more relaxed."

"Great. Now let's do it faster, much faster, five times in a row, letting your mind go blank in between each 'swish.' But first tell me how you make your mind go blank."

Billy stared off into space and said, "I don't know. There's nothing there."

"Do you see black or do you see white, like a snowy TV screen?"

"I see white," he answered.

"Okay, let's begin," I said. "You're going to do five 'swishes' in a row on my hand again. Make sure you do them fast, the way your brain works, with your mind going blank in between."

When he finished, I asked him to put the deep red color on the palm of my hand again.

"I can't," he replied. "But I can see some red around the edges of the blue color that I swished to."

"C'mon," I said. "Make it a pure red color without the blue."

"I can't do it."

"Well, I'm glad," I said. "The fact that you can't see the red by itself indicates to me that the 'swish' worked. Whenever you get angry and it interferes with your golf, just 'swish' the blue over the red as you did today."

"Sounds too easy to me," Billy said. "I've been trying to overcome anger on the golf course for years. And you say I can change it just like that."

"Well, you just did, didn't you? Are you still ready to pack it in?" I asked.

"No, I feel much better," he replied. "Let's go on."

Billy walked to his ball in the rough, chipped up close, and sank his putt for a par. It was obvious that he was pleased with his chip when I saw the broad grin on his face.

Here are the steps for doing "swish" by yourself. The instructions that follow represent a considerably modified and simplified version of Bandler's technique.

''SWISH''

1. Remember a specific time when you felt and acted in a way that interfered with playing well.
2. Identify what you saw and heard at that specific time *just before* your mood changed—a lost-ball slice, perhaps, or stubbed lag putt. As you think about it, *make your images regular pictures* (look through your own eyes, not from a distance).
3. See a color that represents that mood and the way you acted. You may need to see different colors before that mood is properly matched.
4. Identify the kind of state that is *exactly opposite* the undesired one.
5. Remember a specific time on the course when you were in that positive state. Watch yourself acting the

way you want to act *in the form of meta pictures* (watching yourself as if through an outside observer's eyes).

6. See a color in your mind that fully represents that desired mood *and the specific kind of behavior that reflects that mood.* Again, it may be necessary to try different colors to get the most appropriate one.

7. Link the two colors (from steps 3 and 6). In your mind see the first color big and bright and project it onto an imaginary screen in front of you. Then project the second color on top of the first color. The second color should be small and dim and located on the bottom left-hand corner of the first color.

8. Change or "swish" the two colors *quickly* by having the small dim color become big and bright and replace the large first color.

9. Repeat this procedure five times, taking only one second for each repetition. Let your mind go *absolutely blank in between.*

You can test the results in several ways.

1. Project the first color onto your imaginary screen. If it's mostly covered by the second color, the "swish" worked.

2. Project in your mind a future test situation that might result in a negative mood change. Go forward into that situation and discover if you behave in a way you like. (You don't have to smile if you leave the ball in a bunker; just be civil about it.) If the anger changes to curiosity or determination, the "swish" worked.

3. If either of these two tests fails, repeat the whole "swish" process.

SEVEN

The Pro Within: Your Instructional Mind

When you are refining your golf swing, you have two experts to call upon for help: a professional golf teacher and your own mind. Both are important. You need a professionally trained teacher for help in establishing and maintaining proper swing mechanics. You also need to listen to your internal pro.

This was best illustrated by a golfer who, while mentally making a slow-motion image of his swing, noticed that the pictures became blurred at the top of his backswing. He trusted the blurred images as a signal that something there needed correction. Sure enough, his club pro had him shorten his backswing—and better shots soon followed.

This chapter contains techniques you can use to be your own pro, to correct the mechanics of your swing, and to know the difference in mental processing between a good and bad shot. You'll also learn how to improve shots that are rusty, as well as learn how to make new shots without formal instruction.

Getting Good Instruction

It's absolutely essential that you choose a pro who respects and uses the power of *your* mind and turns you back onto your own resources to improve your game. With this attitude a pro can make your learning efficient and enjoyable. The best kind of instruction not only teaches you the fundamentals of the golf swing but guides you to identify and correct your own flaws.

There are hundreds of fine pros. One of the best I know is Willie Carter, from Middletown, New York. He's worked with the best of the touring pros, Gary Player, Tommy Armour, and Orville Moody among them. Willie confirmed to me the legend that he once shot 33 for nine holes using only a 7-iron, scored a 61 for 18 holes using a full bag, and made a hole-in-one on a par-4, 326-yard hole.

Willie emphasizes *swinging* the club, not hitting the ball. He dramatically demonstrates the value of a good swing over the clubs you use by stroking the ball out to the 250-yard sign using one of Gary Player's old putters. Watching *that* can be both a humbling and instructive experience.

Willie simplifies playing golf into a three-count pattern: (1) set up and waggle, (2) swing, and (3) finish and pose to watch the ball. He guides attention to only one or two keys in the first two steps to reduce confusion and brainlock. In step three he insists that you follow every embarrassing dribble until the ball stops rolling, or interrupts the snooze of some jungle creature. During that time Willie directs your mind to "take a lesson." He uses a basic NLP pattern of "reframing"—changing self-criticism of dribbling dubs into appreciation for opportunities to learn.

Taking a lesson during the finish pose becomes easy with

Willie as teacher, because he's a master analyst. He can pick out the single most important elements of the golfer's address position and swing in need of correction, like seeing the blink of a gnat's eye from thirty feet. Then he lets his student know how to identify and correct the error.

Willie is wily on this score. He deliberately lets the golfer experience a swing error several times before he corrects it. Then, as he points out the error and explains the correction, the learner comes to know his mistake well, and especially learns the effects of his correction. As a result the golfer becomes his own chief mechanic later on.

Willie also points out that there are two ways to play a round of golf: One is to practice without regard for score, thinking about one or, at the most, two key elements of the swing, making corrections as you go along; the other way is to play without thinking about swing mechanics—just play—without regard for score except that a record of your strokes is kept. He encourages his pupils to use the latter approach during tournaments.

Willie's approach to learning and playing are consistent with the perspective I have advanced throughout this book—limit your attention to important cues, rely on your own mind to analyze and improve your game, play mindlessly and enjoy yourself. I encourage you to find a pro who shares that perspective also. Willie's approach also reinforces the meta-skills techniques to follow.

The Difference That Makes the Difference

For low handicappers I find that the way they process very small bits of information, visual and auditory, just before or just after they are set up to the ball determines the success or failure of a shot. The pro within can identify the differences between a good and not-so-good shot easily and quickly.

Early one morning one of my doctoral students and I were working with Mike Davis, the assistant pro at Arcola Country Club, on approach shots to an elevated green from about seventy yards out. Mike had just made a poor shot and seemed confused about why it had been bad, especially after he'd been making a lot of good ones just moments before.

So I said to Mike, "Go inside yourself and replay that poor shot in your mind; see, hear, and feel what you saw, heard, and felt on the inside and the outside when you made it. File away in your memory for a minute or two the internal and external A's and V's and K's that were operating as you hit that last bad shot."

Mike closed his eyes and recaptured the memory of the last shot and said, "Okay," implying he was finished.

Then I asked him to do the same thing with one of his great shots to the green five minutes or so earlier. Again he went inside and thought about the good shot.

"Now we're going to find out the difference that makes the difference between those two shots," I said to Mike. "As you think about the A's and V's and K's for each of those shots, what was different about them?"

"The main difference," he answered, "was in seeing the ball. In the bad shot I didn't see the ball clearly; it was fuzzy, similar to the images I had of the ball during the first twelve holes at Willow Ridge."

Earlier, I had had Mike go through this same metaskills technique with a round of golf he had played at Willow Ridge several weeks before. Mike had indicated that he had made a complete reversal in his playing ability from poor play during the first twelve holes, followed by a dramatic improvement in his performance on the 13th hole. We were both curious about what made the difference. The main difference there was the brightness and sharp focus on the ball.

Mike continued saying, "On the good shot the ball was really bright white and it was in focus."

"Now, Mike," I said, "let's test the difference that makes the difference between good and bad approach shots right here, to find out if this difference prevails here as well as at Willow Ridge."

I had him set up to a ball, deliberately defocus, make the ball dull white, and then hit it. The shot was a poor one. Then I told him to sharpen the focus and brighten the ball just before take-away, and hit another shot. The second shot was a fine one.

Mike's conclusion was, "I'm going to add seeing the ball bright and in focus to my preshot checklist. It's really important."

Bill Adams, the Ridgewood pro, discovered that he was "double-crossing" himself when he became confused about what kind of shot to make on an approach. In one instance, comparing a poor approach shot with a good one, the difference that made the difference was in the nature of the images of the intended shot which he made while he was setting up. In the good shot he saw a clear image of the trajectory of the ball and the path of the clubhead; in the poor shot he saw two trajectories superimposed upon each other, one a fade, the other a draw, crossing over each other. When he told me that, I said, "No wonder you messed up that shot; you double-crossed yourself." He had a double-exposed image in his mind's eye at the address position. That would confuse anybody. Do it yourself and find out what happens.

While working with other golfers I found a number of unique differences that made the difference. During his preshot routine one golfer would silently tell himself how he wanted to execute the next shot as he approached the ball.

He discovered that on bad shots his internal voice was harsh in pitch, but on good shots it was melodious. Another golfer was extremely aware of a quiet, internal voice on good shots, and a barking marine sergeant on bad shots. A third golfer heard silence on good shots, and lots of internal debate and chastisement before bad ones.

Here are instructions for determining the difference that makes the difference for you.

DISCOVERING DIFFERENCE

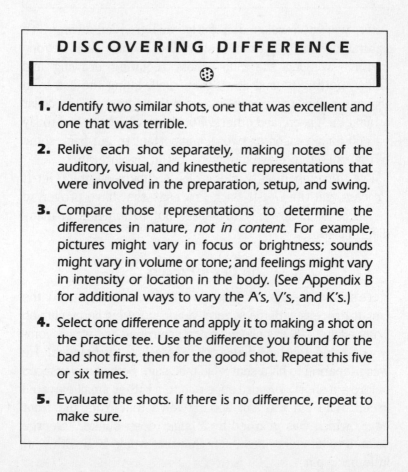

1. Identify two similar shots, one that was excellent and one that was terrible.
2. Relive each shot separately, making notes of the auditory, visual, and kinesthetic representations that were involved in the preparation, setup, and swing.
3. Compare those representations to determine the differences in nature, *not in content.* For example, pictures might vary in focus or brightness; sounds might vary in volume or tone; and feelings might vary in intensity or location in the body. (See Appendix B for additional ways to vary the A's, V's, and K's.)
4. Select one difference and apply it to making a shot on the practice tee. Use the difference you found for the bad shot first, then for the good shot. Repeat this five or six times.
5. Evaluate the shots. If there is no difference, repeat to make sure.

6. If there's a difference, adjust your internal visual and auditory processing to include the difference when you are not playing well.

Developing New Golf Shots

After you've developed a fairly well-grooved swing, it's natural to want to learn new shots that require skills beyond merely swinging the club—shots requiring drawing and fading, getting up and down from sand, lifting the ball from the rough over trees, chipping from thick grass on the collar around the green, and others. For those who have had to lay off golf for a season or two, it's important to get back some of the skills that inevitably were lost in the interim.

I've developed two metaskills techniques—the Get-It Process and the Get-It-Back Process—that have proven to be successful, not only to golfers but to athletes in many different sports.

The Get-It Process

Here's how George Burns, a PGA Tour golfer, used the Get-It Process with me several years ago at his home club on Long Island. He was playing a practice round as I was accompanying and teaching him some metaskills techniques. He was preparing to hit a shot which, he said, he had never faced before—a short, 70-yard approach to a rather small elevated green. The pin was cut about twelve feet from the front edge, which was guarded by a huge, deep bunker. George wanted to hit a very high, soft shot that would land with very little backspin.

I started the process by asking, "Since you've never made this kind of shot before, have you ever watched someone make a similar shot that was superb?"

George gazed into space for a few seconds and said, "Yeah. I saw Nicklaus make one like this."

"Great," I responded. "In your mind go back to the time when you saw Nicklaus make his shot. And put a motion picture of that shot here on the back of my left hand," which I held a couple of feet in front of his face. "As you watch Nicklaus make that shot, feel his swing in your own muscles."

George focused on the back of my hand, moved his club slightly, nodded, looked up, and said, "Okay."

"Now, what I want you to do is to change the picture of Nicklaus to become you, George. See yourself in the clothing you have on now making that shot, and feel your muscles working as you watch yourself stroke the ball."

I remember the day George and I were working. It was cold and windy. He was wearing a rain suit and a winter wool toque. George continued to focus on my hand, nodding. Then I said, "Now change the image from watching yourself from the outside to seeing what you would be seeing if you were right there making the shot. Change the image from a meta picture to a regular picture and see only what you would normally see while setting up and swinging. And really feel the swing throughout your entire body."

After about fifteen or twenty seconds I asked George, "What happened, in your mind, as you did that?"

"I made the shot," he answered.

"Okay. Step up to your ball and reproduce that imagined shot when you're ready."

George reproduced the shot, high, soft, and several feet from the pin. His remark after the shot was "I can't believe it. It really worked."

The Get-It Process doesn't always work on the first go-around, as it did with George. Usually, there are several steps of visualization followed by a change or two in swing mechanics before the golfer "gets it."

To help you understand the extra steps in the process, here's a vignette of my work with Billy Musto, who wanted to get his smooth swing tempo back. The extra steps consisted of combining metaphorical representations of parts of Billy's swing so that they were "chunked" into one swing concept to facilitate concentration. Notice that Billy used the Get-It-Back Process, almost identical to the Get-It Process. I'll make the difference clear as we go along.

The Get-It-Back Process

The day I worked with Billy, I told him to go inside himself and return to a specific time when he was swinging smoothly and hitting the ball well. Billy remembered a specific shot he'd made during a tournament.

I had him put an image of himself making that past, satin-smooth swing on the back of my left hand. I said this was his "criterion" or model I wanted him to reproduce. After Billy went through the process of first watching the movie of his past shot and then watching himself hit the past shot, I had him hit a few balls on the practice tee.

Then I asked him, "Is that what you want?"

"That's not quite it," he replied. "It's a bit too fast at the top and not enough clubhead speed at impact."

"Well, let's take one of those at a time," I said. "Project a movie of what you just did here on the palm of my right hand and compare it to your criterion picture—the way you used to swing—on the back of my left hand. As you study those two pictures or movies, what one, *and only one,* thing do you want to correct in your last shot that you think will get your swing back to where you want it?"

Billy glanced back and forth between my two hands and

said, "The top. I want a slight pause at the top of my backswing before I go into the downswing."

"Just go through that movement now, the take-away to the top, without striking a ball," I said. "And as you do it, let a metaphorical image flash into your mind right at the top of the swing."

Billy took the club back several times, smiled, and said, "I see a swinging traffic light. It's red as it swings in the wind in one direction and then it changes to green as it begins to swing back in the other direction."

"Fine. Test that image in your mind as you swing a club here on the tee without a ball. See if it works."

Billy tested it in his mind and then hit a few balls. Again I asked him, "How'd it go?"

"It's still not right," he replied. "The pause at the top is great. The traffic-light image works, but—"

I interrupted him, believing that he was going to reinforce the negative stuff, something I didn't want him to do. "Make another movie of what you just did with your swing on my right hand and compare it to your criterion on my left. As before, identify *one part* of your swing that you want to correct that'll bring it up to snuff, the way it used to be."

Billy looked at my two hands and said, "I want more clubhead speed down at the ball."

"What can you do to get that?" I asked.

"Just think about whipping the club at the bottom of the downswing and pinching the ball between the face of the club and the turf," he answered.

"Can you think of another metaphorical image related to the traffic light that you could use to generate clubhead speed?"

Billy thought for a moment and, being a sports-car buff, came up with an image of a racing car accelerating out of a curve at the Indianapolis 500, and gunning it an instant before it reached the straightaway.

"Now," I said, "see that metaphorical image in your mind as you swing the club without a ball to find out if it gets what you want in the way of clubhead speed."

He said it did, so I told him to "chunk" the two images—the traffic light and the race car—so they became combined into *one* metaphorical image. He chuckled a bit and said, "I see the red traffic light swinging; it changes to green as it begins to swing back, and then I see a race car down by my right leg come into view, gunning it into the straightaway, past the golf ball. I'm pretty sure it'll work."

Billy made the new, chunked image in his mind as he swung at a ball; it jumped off the club with an audible *click*. He grinned from ear to ear and said, "That's it. That's perfect."

I had him hit several more balls to make sure he had his swing tempo back. He got it back, and now he uses that visual anchor to regulate his swing when it's off; he thinks of nothing when his swing is okay.

Below you will find the steps for the Get-It Process. They are the same for the Get-It-Back Process except for the criterion image or model that you want to get or get back. The criterion for the Get-It is an image of someone else; the criterion for the Get-It-Back is an image of you hitting a golf ball at an earlier time.

Although it's preferable to create metaphors when making corrections in your swing during both the Get-It and the Get-It-Back Process, it's not absolutely necessary. In George Burns's case no metaphor was necessary, since he got it on the first try by reproducing Nicklaus's shot. However, he could have created a metaphor of the shot like Ted Jackson's flying red goose.

Billy Musto, however, used a chunked, visual metaphor in which two were logically put together. This made it easier for him to concentrate. However, he could have succeeded without using any metaphors at all. He could have used only images of mechanical corrections. Whether you make metaphors or not depends upon the ease with which you generate them and the degree to which they facilitate or hinder your progress toward getting it or getting it back. Therefore, you can be flexible in the way you approach the use of metaphorical images.

THE GET-IT PROCESS

This is based on the element of mimicry and the fundamental process of constantly making mental comparisons between what you're actually doing and what you want ideally to do.

1. On the practice range identify a time when you observed a fine golfer, on TV or in person, execute a shot you want to learn.
2. On an imaginary screen flash a movie of that golfer making that intriguing shot.
3. Put yourself into that movie, wearing the clothing you have on now, and feel the movements involved in executing that shot.
4. Change that meta movie into a regular movie (you inside you) and feel the movements of making the shot.
5. Immediately swing and stroke a ball without further preparation. Repeat that shot several times. If you "get it," repeat it several times a day for several weeks, until it becomes automatic.

6. If you don't get it, and most don't the first time, make a meta movie of your last attempt and compare it to the original criterion movie in step 2. Identify by feel the muscle and joint actions needed to make the correction.

7. Execute the shot several more times while paying attention *only* to the one desired correction from step 6. If the shots are satisfactory, you're finished. Practice for the next few weeks until it becomes automatic.

8. Many students still don't get it even after a second try. In that case go back and make another meta movie of your last shot and compare it again to the step-2 original. Ask yourself what *one* correction should be made. Identify the feelings necessary to make the additional correction.

In your mind visualize the shot by "chunking" the two corrections (steps 6 and 8). The idea of chunking is to facilitate concentration on only one correction.

Execute the shot several times more, paying attention *only* to the chunked correction. If that works, *you really are finished.*

Metaphors can be created to anchor the result of the Get-It Process. Here's how to create a metaphorical anchor.

1. When you identify a correction (step 6, above), create a metaphorical representation of it. (Billy Musto used a traffic light.)

2. Execute the shot several times while paying attention *only* to the metaphor. If the shot is satisfactory, the metaphor becomes the anchor.

3. If the first correction is made, but the shot is still unsatisfactory, visually compare it to the criterion and identify another correction. Make a metaphorical representation of this second correction. (Musto chose a racing car.)
4. Visualize making the shot by "chunking" the two corrections into one metaphor. If the shot is satisfactory, the chunked metaphor becomes the anchor.

There is also a Get-It-Back Process. The only difference is the person in the first movie. Instead of that golfer being Nicklaus, or Nancy Lopez, it's you. It's you executing the shot you want to get back, like Billy Musto.

Let's say you want to get a smooth tempo back after a long layoff. Go back to a specific time when your swing was satisfactory. Relive it with the image of yourself making that flowing pass at the ball. Continue with the Get-It Process starting at step 3.

Holographic Viewing

Holographic Viewing is a systematic process of imagery that registers a proper swing pattern in your neuromuscular system, in the brain-nerve-muscle connections that make a golf swing happen. It consists of watching a good athlete from different positions "around the clock." That is, you can watch a good golfer on the practice tee from the front, back, sides, and positions in between, as long as you can keep out of the way of the ball.

Holographic Viewing is quite precise. Immediately after

you watch a golfer swing, close your eyes and make an internal movie that reproduces it. Consciously feel your muscles become active while looking at the movie. When you're reasonably certain your internal movie accurately reproduces the golfer's swing, move to a different position and watch him swing again. Make another internal movie and feel the swing in your muscles as before. Repeat this process until you have viewed your model golfer perform the same shot from various positions "around the clock."

Now you have a set of criterion movies of a swing that you want to match in the Get-It Process described earlier. Not only do you have a model to copy, but you have already put into your brain much of the neural activity needed for you to reproduce the desired swing.

The imagery techniques presented in this chapter can be used for any kind of shot; they will be particularly useful in developing new ones. Putting yourself in Paul Azinger's body in the sand and Ben Crenshaw's on the green might not put you on the pro tour, but it's worth the effort to improve your swing.

Paradoxical Intention

One evening I received a call from a client—a professional—who was depressed about his performance in a tournament. He was discouraged with his usual habit of getting bogeys and double bogeys on the first couple of holes, followed by pars and an occasional birdie on the remaining holes. He wanted to change that programed scoring pattern.

This is what I told him to do: An hour or so before his tee-off time he hit several buckets of balls on the practice range; I told him to *deliberately* hit lousy shots—shots that he would normally hit during early tournament play when his swing pattern was disrupted. While doing this he paid attention to how he controlled his bad shots—what he did in his mind and how he swung.

After about five minutes of hitting poor shots he corrected them by paying attention to his normal swing keys. With this process he learned how to make corrections readily. The result of this paradoxical practice routine was a consistently good scoring pattern with only an occasional lapse in his swing during competition. When those lapses now occur during tournaments, he has the ability to correct them quickly.

This seemingly odd process is called paradoxical intention. The way out of a bad behavior pattern is to go further into it so you not only understand how you goof, but you also gain control of goofing. When you develop the power to goof deliberately, you have increased control over your behavior, and you build confidence, too. In this way it becomes relatively easy for low and middle handicappers to learn how to correct defective swings. Shades of Willie Carter's instructional process—sound familiar?

EIGHT

Swing Effort: The Short Game

You have gotten to the green, or come fairly close, but can see no reason for joy. That's because you've been there before, and realize all too well that the final dozen yards of a hole can be harder than the first few hundred. On the half swings and gentle pings so necessary on those shots, you've been halfhearted. This chapter focuses on the mind games of the short game. Without a good short game, power hitters off the tee become scoring weaklings. And even if they get on the green in regulation, the "yips" can bring them to their knees. Although metaskills techniques for this aspect of golf come from deep within the nervous system, they can be easily learned.

Effort Control

What is central to shots taken from off and on the green? A bunch of clichés heard on the course point to the answer: "bite," "get legs," "one more turn," "I babied it," "too many

Wheaties," "never up, never in." The key to the short game is effort, the exact amount needed to get the ball either close to the pin or in the hole.

Regulating the amount of swing effort is the least understood mental task in golf. I've reviewed golf books and videotapes on the short game and haven't found any useful instructions about how hard to hit the ball. Nor do the authors tell you how to establish the line of a putt or chip. They tell you to *visualize* the shots, how to hold the club, how to stand, and how to swing, but they don't tell you *how* to visualize a shot or *how* to determine the necessary amount of effort to apply to your swing. This is what you're about to learn.

It's no wonder that we've known so little about how to regulate swing effort in golf. It's an amazingly complex process because so many variables are involved. External variables include: distance between the ball and the pin, wind speed and direction, intervening hazards, the lie of the ball, the nature of the ground on which the golfer stands, and the contour and degree of firmness of the green.

Internal variables include: strength, ability to swing the club in particular ways, emotional state, sensitivity to muscular pressure and tension, visual acuity, and the way you mentally process and integrate all the relevant information. It's absolutely impossible to do all this consciously, so let's learn how to turn it over to your unconscious mind with its automatic neuromuscular connections.

The Fundamental Principle

The fundamental idea that determines swing effort is that vision is integrated with muscle action; the V's and K's go together. Obviously, hitting golf balls to targets must involve a combination of seeing and feeling. By looking at the target—the landing area, the contour of the green, a spot on a green, or the flagstick—the golfer ends up with a sense of which club to use, how far to open the face of a lofted club, and how hard to hit the ball. To learn how to combine visual and kinesthetic information requires knowing what to pay attention to so that the production of the right swing effort gets the ball to the target.

What Do Expert Golfers Pay Attention To?

How do "fine-touch" players know how much swing effort to use on approaches and chips? How do they read greens and know how hard to strike putts? Rather like tapping into a rich mine, I was able to dig this information out of the minds of a few golfers by using NLP strategy-elicitation procedures referred to in an earlier chapter.

When I asked a number of short-game wizards how they controlled their shots around and on the greens, they all said they knew from *experience.* Some said they imagined *(saw)* the trajectory, bounce, and roll of approach shots, and could see the speed of putts rolling on a path right into the hole; others said they *felt* the shots. Upon further questioning it became clear that they did a lot of other important things unconsciously, which they eventually verified after I rooted around in their brains.

The fundamental principle of combining visual and kinesthetic information was repeatedly verified. All the pros start with visual information to get the right swing feeling. Bill Adams, the pro at Ridgewood, first looks at the target to identify the slope and contour of the green and the distance to the pin. Then he sees in his mind's eye the trajectory that he wants the ball to follow to the hole, based on his memory of the trajectories of past shots.

Then Bill reverses the process, moving in his mind from feeling to seeing. For instance, when chipping, after he feels the firmness of the green underfoot to get a sense of how fast the ball will roll, he swings his club to gain a sense of its heft. As he swings with different amounts of effort, pictures of a flight and roll of the ball are created on his mental screen. The images equate the amount of swing effort he feels in his arms and wrists. He compares these internal pictures to the desired trajectory, roll, and speed of the ball which he had previously established. When his internal picture appears to match the desired imagined shot, he tests the match between image and swing effort again by feeling the speed of his swing and seeing internal pictures.

When he senses that the match is just right, he reproduces the desired swing effort with several more practice swings. In his mind he again creates a moving picture of the ball as it leaves the club face and rolls into the hole. He says it's important for him to see the club face strike the ball in his mental image; if he doesn't, his chip will be bad, either too strong or too weak, because he can't be sure how sharply to hit the ball.

Finally, when his internal pictures match, when he sees the complete flight of the ball, and when he has the right feeling of the swing effort in his arms, wrists, and hands, Bill trusts his preparation, steps up to the ball, and hits it without any conscious thoughts in his mind at all. Clearly, Bill's expertise comes from knowing what to look at, what to feel when he swings the club, and how to translate all that information into the just-right swing effort. Let's look more closely at the crucial information a golfer needs to know about swing effort and how you can acquire it.

Crucial Visual Information

Two kinds of visual information are crucial for controlling swing effort: the information you see on the outside and the internal images that are either remembered or created on the spot. Both kinds of information are processed at the same time. It's all of this visual information taken together that tells the golfer how hard to strike the ball.

Many golfers have a stored visual chart in their minds that contains a list of their clubs and the amount of yardage they can hit with each of them under normal conditions. They also have yardage figures related to wind and wet conditions that they subtract from or add to the normal yardage; some have a figure related to feeling pumped up that is factored in too. With the more skilled golfers this information about the weather and their feeling states is automatically cranked into their decision about club selection and how hard to swing.

Estimating distance is obviously a visual process. For example, many golfers have ten-yard, twenty-five-yard, and fifty-yard visual templates stored in their minds that they use to estimate the distance of approach shots; for putting they have three-foot and ten-foot templates. They project and superimpose these templates onto the ground, using either the 150-yard markers, the ball itself, or the flagstick as the initial points from which to calculate the distance to the hole.

If they're not sure, they'll actually step off the distance. Tour golfers or their caddies walk a tournament course before the first round, chart the location of water sprinkler heads, hazards, and trees, and record their distances to the front of each green. In addition, they check pin placements before each round and record their distances from the front of the green.

Planning the trajectory or flight of the ball over intervening hazards such as sand traps, rough, knolls, and even trees is important for landing the ball close to or on the putting surface. The loft of the club, the address position, and the degree of openness of the club face are other bits of visual information that are cranked into the decision about how fast to swing the clubhead.

After distance and trajectory are ascertained, certain internal visual information related to past, similar approaches and chips is retrieved from their memories; this also serves as a basis for making a decision about how hard to strike the ball. Significant remembered visual information about past shots includes: the club used, the line or trajectory of the ball, the position of the club face in relation to the pin or hole at the end of the swing, and the trajectory, bounce, and roll of the ball to its resting spot. All of this visual information helps the golfer select the right club and gives him a good idea of the required swing effort.

Establishing the Line of a Putt

After the ball is on the green, the major task is to determine the line of the putt. Golfers spend a great deal of time pacing, squatting, plumbing, and eyeballing the contours of the green while lining up a putt. Although this might seem a bit much to the uninitiated, it's necessary to identify the likely path that the ball will take to the hole—the roll line—and to establish the target line, the direction which the ball will *initially* follow on its way to the hole. The direction of the first few feet of the target line determines the target spot to which the golfer aims. The target spot may be located at or near the hole, or at a point closer to the ball. This spot will vary from putt to putt depending on the distance the ball is from the cup, the contour of the green, and the golfer's swing effort.

The most important visual information you must have to

determine the roll line of a putt is the remembered images of how golf balls have rolled under similar conditions. Obviously, the best way to gain experience in guessing how a golf ball will roll on a green is to watch hundreds of golf balls roll on greens of varied contour until you have an eye for such phenomena.

This can be done in several ways. One is to watch skilled golfers putt, using the Get-It Process (see page 94). The important steps in this process are those related to feeling, in your own muscles, the amount of effort the skilled golfer appears to use when he strikes the ball.

A second way is to putt hundreds of golf balls on all sorts of differently contoured greens and watch their roll lines, noticing the speed of the roll and feeling the effort you use as you strike the ball. It's absolutely essential that you associate your swing effort with the roll line, because fast-moving balls will follow a line different from slow-moving balls. Fast-moving balls are less affected by the green's contour and bumps than slow-moving balls.

The "Third" Eye

Bill Burgess, the head pro at Arcola, uses an imaginary "third eye," located on the left side of his head, to keep the distance, roll line, and swing effort in mind all at once as he sets up to putt. When he is set up, he peers at the ball and beams an image of the roll line leading to the hole with his "third eye." In his mind this image is projected onto an imaginary screen located several feet to his left on a line connecting him and the hole. This third-eye image also keeps his head down and steady when he's over the ball.

The metaskills technique of "Greenprinting" is useful for "reading" putts. It's similar to creating a mental blueprint. It can be practiced during a practice round of golf. Here are the steps.

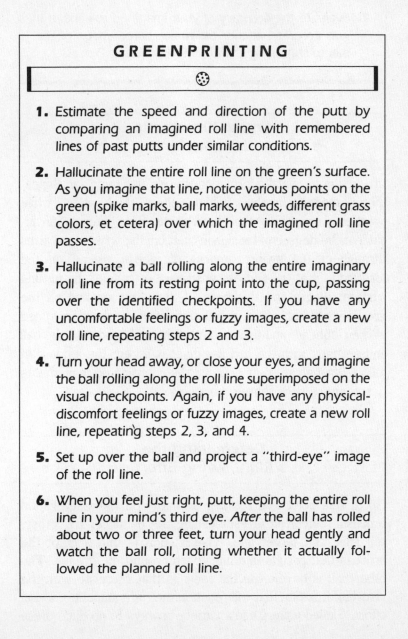

GREENPRINTING

1. Estimate the speed and direction of the putt by comparing an imagined roll line with remembered lines of past putts under similar conditions.

2. Hallucinate the entire roll line on the green's surface. As you imagine that line, notice various points on the green (spike marks, ball marks, weeds, different grass colors, et cetera) over which the imagined roll line passes.

3. Hallucinate a ball rolling along the entire imaginary roll line from its resting point into the cup, passing over the identified checkpoints. If you have any uncomfortable feelings or fuzzy images, create a new roll line, repeating steps 2 and 3.

4. Turn your head away, or close your eyes, and imagine the ball rolling along the roll line superimposed on the visual checkpoints. Again, if you have any physical-discomfort feelings or fuzzy images, create a new roll line, repeating steps 2, 3, and 4.

5. Set up over the ball and project a "third-eye" image of the roll line.

6. When you feel just right, putt, keeping the entire roll line in your mind's third eye. *After* the ball has rolled about two or three feet, turn your head gently and watch the ball roll, noting whether it actually followed the planned roll line.

7. Evaluate the accuracy of your imagined roll line. If it was accurate, anchor the remembered image of the ball rolling, using the Uptime Anchoring Process.

Crucial Kinesthetic Information

In addition to visual information there's also important kinesthetic information that skillful golfers think about while practicing or playing the short game. This information includes: the degree of tension in their hands, wrists, and arms throughout the swing; amount of weight placed on the forward foot at the address position; firmness of the putting surface; length and thickness of the grass on and off the green; wind; heft of the club; length of the backswing; speed of the clubhead; and the contact of the clubhead with the ball and perhaps with the turf if a divot is taken; the amount of follow-through after impact; and the coordinated movements of the entire body during the swing.

Determining the Right Swing Effort

Up to this point I've focused primarily on the visualization processes involved in establishing the distance, trajectory, roll line, and target line. Visualization is only half of the process that results in a fine touch around the greens. The other half is developing the feelings that correlate with the visual information that will result in the right amount of swing effort. Skilled golfers use a variety of ways to produce these swing feelings, the feelings that I refer to as swing effort. The following are ways that some professional golfers do this. You, too, can follow their lead when you practice.

Imaginary Ball Toss

Some fine chippers and putters pretend they're tossing or rolling a ball underhand toward the pin or hole with what they presume to be the right amount of effort. During the toss they see an imaginary ball fly through the air and roll toward the hole. If the imaginary ball doesn't reach the hole or goes too far, they repeat the tossing motion until there is a match between the effort of the arm swing and the imagined trajectory and roll that gets the ball to the hole.

In the next step the same amount of effort is reproduced while making a practice swing with the appropriate club. Like Bill Adams, you, too, can let an image of the ball's trajectory and roll be generated in your mind as you make practice swings. When the two images match—the tossing image and the swing image—step up to the ball and stroke it with the same amount of swing effort.

Getting the Feel of the Greens

Pre-round chipping and putting practice on the practice green will help to determine the conditions of the greens on the course to some extent. This will give you a sense of how hard you must strike the ball to get it to roll a certain distance. Feeling the sponginess of each green as you walk near the intended roll line of your ball will also give you an idea of the speed of an impending putt.

Peter Kostis recommends that you get a feel for the speed of a green by observing the swing effort of your playing partners as they swing and roll the ball to the cup. Steps of the Get-It Process are useful here.

Putting Energy

There's controversy among professional golfers about whether to putt the ball firmly or let it die at the hole. I don't think it matters on long level putts. However, there are some very short downhill breaking putts that are best struck firmly so the ball strikes the liner at the back the cup. If struck softly the break becomes more of a major factor, requiring much more finesse and V-K information processing than necessary; the slower the ball rolls, the more its direction is influenced by the contour, bumps, and cleat marks. On the other hand, *long* downhill breaking putts are probably best accomplished by a soft and slow-rolling putt; it's less likely to result in two more putts from far, far away.

To make the amount of energy applied to the blade of your putter consistent, the placement of your hands on the club should be the same at all times. When you increase the distance between your hands and the blade, assuming all other aspects of your swing remain constant, the faster the clubhead will swing because the length of the lever arm is increased, and the further the ball will roll. If you maintain the same hand position on the club for all putts, there will be less need to modify muscle tension in your arms, wrists, and shoulders, because the length of the lever arm will remain constant. As a result you'll have a keener sense of the swing effort needed to make various putts.

Several professional golfers have told me that they partially regulate their swing effort for the short game *and* putting by the length of their backswing. The longer the backswing, the more effort at impact. This seems to be a useful process for chips and approach shots. However, as I've watched scores of professionals putt, there is no correlation between the backswing and the speed of a putt.

They *think* they are taking the club back further on longer putts, when in reality they are not.

When I challenge them about this notion, they realize that it's the firmness of their grip, the tension in their forward leg at impact, and the energy they apply during the forward part of the putting stroke that determines the speed of the club-head and the speed of the ball.

Finally, it's helpful to have a sense of your own energy level as you strike the ball. As you well know, some days you feel strong and supple and your swing requires very little effort. On other days, when you feel sluggish and tight as a rusty bolt, more effort—and maybe a little WD-40—is needed to get the ball moving. Pre-round practice will let you know your current energy level.

How to Develop the Short-Game Touch

Obviously, practice is the fundamental answer to the question of how to create the right swing effort; and a facile memory for past good shots helps too. But how, specifically, do fine-touch golfers practice, and what do they actually do in their minds to snuggle a ball up close to the pin, or sink it with that familiar and pleasing *plunk*?

For approach shots, including chips, many professional golfers often hit thousands of balls to circles marked on the practice range or green that are a predeterminded number of yards away. Putting practice is approached in much the same way from predetermined distances on varied slopes.

Some professionals practice putting by placing a number of balls on a straight line and putting them a specified distance to a parallel line marked with chalk on the green. Bill Adams uses a "ladder drill," stroking a ball to say six feet, then eight feet, then ten feet, and so on. Others, like Greg Norman, putt for the hole at different distances. It's reported that he putts twenty-five balls placed in a circle around a hole beginning at a distance of three feet. When he sinks them all, he moves out one foot. It's said that he has reached a distance of eight feet from the hole without missing—150 successful putts in a row!

During practice many professionals attend to only one or two cues at a time, as in the Uptime Anchor. They spend several minutes concentrating on the softness of their hands while holding the club, then on weight balance, then on follow-through, and so on, all in relation to how much effort it takes to get the ball to the hole. In this way they anchor swing effort to individual visual and kinesthetic cues.

This kind of practice can engrave in your memory the sights and feelings of hitting each ball. Deliberately associate, for each distance and slope, the feelings in your hands, arms, and legs during the swing with the trajectory, roll, speed, and final resting spot of each ball.

Gradually, you will become adept at the short game, spending less and less time hitting balls at predetermined distances from the hole. Of course, you will still have to practice regularly, but eventually you can limit your practice time because your sense of touch will have become thoroughly honed. The ultimate outcome of practice is to get the right feelings in your muscles for playing better golf.

The V-K Weave

The V-K Weave is a technique for developing the right amount of swing effort for chipping and putting. It helps you to weave seeing and swing effort together strongly. Oddly and paradoxically, it involves chipping and putting with your eyes closed. Here's how it goes.

V-K WEAVE

1. During practice, with your eyes open, chip several balls from a short distance off the green. Pay close attention to the amount of muscle tension that existed in your arms, forearms, and forward leg during the swing that got one of the balls close to the hole.

2. Put another ball in the same place as the earlier chip. While taking a practice swing feel, in your mind, the exact same amount of muscle tension and swing effort that you felt on the previous successful shot.

3. Hit the ball, reproducing the swing effort and muscle feelings of the prior successful shot. As soon as you see the clubhead strike the ball, close your eyes.

4. Keeping your eyes closed *and remaining keenly aware of the muscle feelings,* make an internal picture of the ball going to the hole.

5. Estimate how close to the hole you think the ball came to rest—within two feet of the pin, shorter than two feet, or longer than two feet—based on the degree of muscle tension you felt while swinging the club.

6. Open your eyes and see where the ball actually came to rest. Anchor the shot in your Uptime Anchor if it came within two feet of the pin.

7. Repeat the entire process several times for chip shots taken from different locations around the green, anchoring only the successful ones.

The V-K Weave can also be used for a variety of approaches and for long putts. The fundamental idea is to learn how to peg the amount of swing effort used while hitting a variety of shots. Closing your eyes forces you to attend consciously to muscle feelings. After you become adept at this, let this mental process drop into your unconscious mind, bringing it back to conscious awareness only when your approaches and putts are missing the mark.

The Emotions of the Short Game

The most important K, for the short game especially, is the just-right feeling state for the shot at hand. When that feeling isn't present, good golfers step away from the ball and plan the shot again. I believe the "yips"—feeling nervous and stabbing at a putt instead of stroking it—are the result of not knowing your just-right putting state *and* not making use of your nervous, uncomfortable feelings.

Valerie, a middle-handicapper, complained of having the "yips," often missing short, easy putts. I asked her to remember a recent putt and describe the feeling she had when standing over the ball. She said she had a feeling of tension in her stomach; and when she putted, she poked at the ball, zipping it past the hole.

I asked Valerie to use the Sherlock Holmes Exercise to get more details about that putt out of her unconscious mind. After she became Sherlock, she realized that she had misread the line and felt uncertain about how to hit the ball; she didn't trust the line. She said the feeling of stomach tension appeared at the same time she felt uncertain.

"You had a vital piece of information available to you and

you ignored it," I told her. "Your unconscious mind was telling you, in the form of an uncomfortable feeling in your stomach, that something wasn't right. Had you trusted your distrust about the line, and had you trusted your feeling of uncertainty about the putt, you could have conquered the 'yips.' You could have stepped away from the ball and prepared to putt differently, with a new line and perhaps a different swing effort. Instead, you went ahead and putted anyway and created a just-wrong anchor."

To suggest that the "yips" were something to be used constructively, rather than just ignored, was a switch. Most people say, "Don't think about them. Just trust your ability and go ahead and putt." My experience suggests that that perspective is foolish *when you are uncertain* about a shot to begin with. Only when you feel certain, or at least comfortable with the way you've planned the shot, should you put trust in your putting skill.

Some people buy new putters to increase their confidence and overcome the "yips." This doesn't make sense for a couple of reasons. First, a different putter won't correct the way you've been reading the greens and determining a swing effort. Second, building another memory bank of associations between the speed of putts and the length and weight of a new putter will take a great deal of extra practice time; and it may even aggravate the problem.

The "yips" are a signal that your performance strategy is out of whack. Something's messed up in your mental program that's interfering with taking the proper stance and generating the proper swing effort. When the programed performance strategy gets back in gear, the "yips" will fade away.

The Short Game During Competition

Throughout this book I have emphasized the importance of thinking about nothing when you hit the ball. This holds true for all parts of the short game, too, even though there's a great deal of thought that goes into planning approaches, chips, and putts *before* you address the ball.

The *practice* techniques I have described for determining swing effort are all *conscious* techniques. When you're playing a competitive round, conscious mental processing should be considerably reduced. It's still important to consciously plan the trajectory, roll line, target line, and target spot so you can generate the feeling of the swing effort. But if you've practiced these techniques in advance, they can be done quickly during your preshot routine while waiting for your playing partners to hit their balls.

To do this take a couple of practice swings before you set up to the ball, while you're waiting for the others in your foursome to hit. If it's your turn to hit first, do this quickly to avoid slow play. With each swing visualize the flight or roll of the ball from club face to target, and feel the amount of swing effort to get the ball to the pin. If the image of the ball's flight and feeling of the swing effort don't fit together, then change the swing and the image until they do. In other words, the practice swing is actually a rehearsal swing. Then, and only then, step up to the ball and swing mindlessly.

If you've done your homework—if you've thoroughly practiced reading greens, if you've etched in your mind and muscles the look and feel of shots from different distances—then mental preparation during a round of golf can be done quickly and easily. Just step up and swing without any further thought at all. That's the time to trust your unconscious mind. But if you feel doubtful, trust your feeling of uncertainty and quickly replan the shot, allowing whatever anchors you've created (e.g., music, color, metaphors, images, movements) to take over automatically.

Summary

Here are some reminders and suggestions for regulating swing effort. They are organized according to desired outcomes and can serve as a ready reference when you are deciding what to practice.

EFFORT CONTROL

Estimating Distance

- Create a club-distance chart and practice seeing it in your mind.
- Create imaginary distance templates. Check their accuracy by stepping off the distance during practice rounds.

Reading Greens

- Check the firmness of greens underfoot.
- Observe the trajectory and roll of many good shots by yourself and others.
- Use the Get-It Process to estimate the swing effort of playing partners as a basis for determining the speed of a green.

Determining Energy Level

- Analyze distance of pregame practice shots.

Determining Trajectory and Line

- Use Greenprinting.
- Use practice swings to generate an imaginary trajectory and roll for each shot.
- Imagine a ball's entire trajectory and roll from club face to hole while taking practice swings.

Determining Club Speed

- Use Imaginary Ball Toss to estimate the strength needed to swing club faster.
- Use the Uptime Anchor to identify the feelings of balance, grip strength, length of backswing and follow-through, and sharpness of impact that are associated with different distances, trajectories, and roll lines.

Determining Swing Effort

- Determine your energy level at the start of each round.
- Maintain a consistent hand position on the club.
- Develop the mental skill of the "third eye."
- Anchor the swing effort of various types of shots with metaphors, music, color, images, sounds, and movements.
- Use the V-K Weave.

Eliminating the "Yips."

- Use the Sherlock Holmes Exercise to identify what happens in your mind *just before* you have the "yips" or sense of doubt. Change your internal strategy to eliminate the uncomfortable feeling of the "yips."
- Trust your feelings of uncertainty when you address the ball; step back and replan the shot if you feel discomfort.

NINE

Self-hypnosis: Tapping the Power of Your Unconscious Mind

Tony Jacklin, the former British and United States Open golf champion, has reported that during a few rounds of golf he experienced "a cocoon of concentration" in which everything was "pure, vividly clear." During one of those states he hit a 350-yard drive. Essentially, Jacklin's state was a trance state during which there was little or no deliberate conscious thought.

My investigations of athletes' mental states during competition reveal that they're frequently in a deep trance state when they perform their best.

For example, Tom Purtzer, a PGA Tour veteran, automatically puts himself into a trance or mindless state by staring at the printing on the surface of the golf ball as he sets up. Peter Famiano, PGA professional at Crestmont Golf Club in West Orange, New Jersey, simply alters his state by staring at one dimple on the golf ball. And David Graham hears his internal voice saying, "Good shot, good shot, good shot," as he takes the clubhead back; this phrase functions as a mantra and hypnotizes him during his swing.

In golf a trance state usually occurs during the time between take-away and when the club strikes the ball, although it may last longer, as in Jacklin's case. Scott, a golf professional at a club outside of Washington, D.C., told me he experienced a trance state throughout his best-ever game. He said, "It was as if I wasn't there." Even as he was reporting the experience to my writing partner and me, he demonstrated physical symptoms of a light trance: defocused, glassy eyes, relaxed facial muscles, and slowed-up speech.

This kind of experience is not limited to professional golfers. Ann Dickimson, a middle-handicapper from Ridgewood, New Jersey, said she experienced an entire round of golf when she was in a zone that allowed her to play at top form. A few of my golfing acquaintances have also reported that sometimes they play an entire round of golf without thinking any thoughts whatsoever about the mechanics of setting up and swinging; it's as if some other part of them is swinging the club, they say, another indication of an altered state of consciousness.

Some athletes who have competed in contests while in trance states have told me that time was distorted to the point that movements appeared to be executed in extremely slow motion. One golfer said he could actually see the spin of the ball just after he struck it. Bill Burgess, if you recall, said that he saw strings and geometric patterns that were directly related to the path of the club and the trajectory of the ball. Others, many others, have said that they knew a shot would be good even *before* they hit it. How many times have *you* absolutely known a shot or putt would be good before you actually hit it?

In contrast to positive trance states there are many golfers who generate negative trance states through intense self-criticism. They are constantly in a depressed state. I'm sure you've played with people like this. They're the ones who are always talking to themselves, silently and out loud, repeatedly saying, "You jerk, your swing stinks," "All you do is slice the ——— ball," "You can't putt worth ——— " Essentially, they generate unconscious negative imagery and muscle feelings, and form a negative perception of themselves that often becomes a self-fulfilling prophecy. Needless to say, their golf shots go all over the lot when they're in that state.

The Nature of Trance

Many people have a mistaken notion about trancc, believing that it's a mystical phenomenon, attainable only by some people. It's not. Getting into a trance is a natural skill, not a trait, contrary to the opinion of some hypnosis specialists. Those who assert that some people are not hypnotizable are mistaken. The late Dr. Milton H. Erickson, a renowned medical hypnotherapist whose work served as one foundation stone of Neuro-Linguistic Programming, was one of the first to recognize the naturalness of trance; and he incorporated it into his remarkably unique and successful practice.

All people have the ability to induce a trance state in themselves—to change their state of consciousness. It's just a matter of taking time to redevelop the appropriate mental processes. Like children we have the innate capacity to become instantly enraptured by the simplest of experiences, but overemphasis on rationality by our educational system has dampened our respect for the unconscious.

Children naturally become deeply engrossed in the simple pleasures of watching birds and kites soar in the sky, of listening to buzzing bees as they hover over flowers to extract their nectar, of losing track of time and space before the television screen, all the while becoming transported away from the here-and-now into their world of fantasy and right-brain mental activity.

Adults, too, know what it's like to alter their states of consciousness but frequently forget that they know. Like children, they're awed by sunsets, transformed by music, enchanted by novels and stories, absorbed in thought while waiting for a traffic light to change, and their moods are altered by hundreds of everyday experiences in a matter of seconds. Trances are induced by riding in elevators, driving long distances on interstate highways, listening to the clickety-clack of the wheels on railroad tracks, making love, intensely focusing on a golf ball, and recalling the details of a past superb golf shot as if they were Sherlock Holmes.

Putting Hypnosis to Work

Having studied and experimented with hypnosis in athletics, I'm convinced that it's perhaps the most powerful tool athletes can use to regulate the consistency of their performance. Essentially, hypnosis is a process of creating, intensifying, and stabilizing an inner-directed state of consciousness. Most of my metaskills techniques are based on this process, and are designed to tap the resources of the unconscious mind by distracting and quieting the conscious mind.

The Sherlock Holmes Exercise induces and stabilizes the hypnotic phenomenon of age regression—going back to a former time and place in your life. The M & M Process, anchoring, and various forms of imagery also stimulate hypnotic processes. Metaphors in particular, like storytelling, generate states most conducive to fine athletic performance. Metaskills techniques activate the nondominant hemisphere of the brain, precisely the part of the brain that is fully activated during trance. These trance states open the door for expanding our world of inner experiences, which are essential for making changes in outward behavior.

Several athletes with whom I have worked have experimented with performing *simple, safe skills* after hypnotizing themselves. They invariably report that their performance becomes almost effortless. One club professional I know said that he has hit some of the best shots in his life while in a self-induced altered state. Through self-hypnosis he also reduced the pressure he normally put on himself to turn in low scores. He says he now enjoys his rounds of golf more and regularly turns in halfway decent scores. For him halfway decent is 75.

Self-hypnosis

For you to hypnotize yourself requires a certain mind-set to begin with. Essentially, you let yourself go and give yourself permission to experience your inner world fully, gradually becoming less and less aware of external reality, as in Zen meditation. Just let your mind go in a consciously determined or suggested direction, yet allow it to generate whatever sensory representations it wants to with absolutely no conscious control. This means letting go of ordinary ways of thinking, adopting an attitude of curiosity and a desire to learn from the hypnotic experience.

I have taught hundreds of athletes a simple form of self-hypnosis. After it is learned, you can use it to tap internal resources and achieve important outcomes. The technique was developed by Betty Erickson, Dr. Erickson's wife. I have modified it slightly. It's really quite simple.

Read over the instructions below and the descriptions of

the reactions of people who have experienced the technique. This will answer some of your questions about what to expect from being in an altered state. Later, when you feel comfortable about hypnotizing yourself, memorize the steps in the process, follow them, and go into an altered state.

The Betty Erickson Technique (modified)

Sit comfortably in a quiet place where you won't be disturbed. Separate your legs slightly, with your forearms and hands resting comfortably on your thighs. Support your head by resting it against the back of a chair or against the wall.

Step 1—Meta Picture

With your eyes open or closed make a meta picture of yourself seated as you are. When you have a clear meta picture of yourself, gently close your eyes and hold that picture for a few seconds.

Step 2—See, Hear, and Feel

Now, *with your eyes closed, see* pictures in your mind of any *three* objects in the room; *hear* any *three* sounds in the surrounding environment such as a ticking clock or traffic noises outside; and *feel* any *three* things on the surface of your body. Then see any *two* things, hear any *two* sounds, and feel any *two* physical sensations, as before. And then see *one* thing, hear *one* thing, and feel *one* thing.

Step 3—Go to a Place of Pleasure

Now become aware of one hand and arm getting heavier than the other. You can press that hand down against your thigh. The lighter arm may begin to bend and your hand may lift itself upward. The movement will be ever so slow, jerky, and automatic. In your mind go to a place of pleasure, a place where you've been before and where you have thoroughly enjoyed yourself. See, hear, and feel again what you saw, heard, and felt before in that special place of yours. Enjoy again the experiences you had there.

At some point during this recollection of pleasure, you'll begin to notice that your rate and depth of breathing has changed, your heart rated has changed, and your sense of the weight of your arms and legs has changed. You might also discover that one of your hands has lifted. When you notice any of these changes, use them as a signal for you to let your mind go wherever it wants to go, becoming passively curious about what will happen next.

Step 4—Back to "Normal"

At some point your unconscious mind will give you a signal—in the form of a personally meaningful internal image, sound, or bodily sensation—that implies that it's time to begin to return to your original normal state. For instance, if your hand rose during the process, its slow movement downward is a signal to return to normal.

Rouse yourself gradually by opening your eyes, looking at the objects around you, listening to the sounds in the environment, and moving parts of your body. Be sure that you are fully alert before you engage in an activity that could result in an injury.

Reactions to Self-hypnosis

I've taught this form of self-hypnosis to many groups of athletes. The following is an account of the reactions of one group immediately after they had experienced an altered state using the Betty Erickson Technique. At the end of the session the group gradually returned to the here-and-now. It took about two or three minutes for everyone to reorient themselves.

"I'm curious to know what reactions, questions, and comments you have about your hypnotic experience," I asked the group when they all appeared to be alert.

Kathryn initiated the response by saying, "I felt as if I'd been asleep, but I know I was listening to your voice and following your suggestions."

Another reaction came from Bruce. "It was different for me. Once my arm started to lift, I just tuned you out altogether. I was in my own world."

In contrast, Maria said, "I was so surprised when my arm started to lift. I kept peeking at it, wondering if there was something wrong with me because it didn't go up at first. But I finally ignored it, and then it started up all by itself."

"I was really disappointed when my arm didn't come up," Gordon commented. "When you said that I didn't have to listen to your voice, I noticed that I got very warm and my arms and legs felt very heavy. It was a pleasant, relaxed feeling. That was certainly a different state from when I started the exercise."

Peter reported his experience by saying, "I was sure surprised when I didn't experience the deep relaxation that I've heard should happen during hypnosis. Instead, I felt quite excited."

"My guess," I told him, "is that you were reexperiencing an exciting event in that special place of pleasure."

"That's right," he agreed. "I was riding a huge wave in the surf at the seashore."

Then I asked if any of them had *not* gone into an altered state.

"I didn't," Cheryl answered. "I tried to get relaxed, but it just didn't work."

"That's okay," I said. "This technique might not be the best way for you. Perhaps you didn't follow the instructions. You said that you '*tried* to relax.' That's a difficult thing to do. Trying to relax is like trying to be spontaneous, or trying to go to sleep. Those three states—relaxation, spontaneity, and sleep—just happen; they can't be engineered."

For anyone who has an experience similar to Cheryl's, I suggest that you do the exercise several more times. It you're still unsuccessful, it doesn't mean you are unhypnotizable. It merely means that another form of hypnosis, tailored to your individual way of processing sensory information, is necessary. Deciding the most useful form, however, requires some individual attention by a qualified clinician.

Loren, another member of the group, had looked uncomfortable during the hypnosis session, opening her eyes several times during the exercise. "If you're willing to talk about it," I said, "would you tell us about your experience?"

"I didn't want to do it at all," she replied. "Frankly, I was afraid. I didn't want to lose control."

"I'm glad you chose not to," I responded. "When you have more trust in me, perhaps you'll be willing to experience it.

"To learn this technique requires that you give up a certain amount of control by your conscious mind and let yourself go, the way I want you to hit a golf ball—mindlessly. It means that you will trust the process and your unconscious mind to take care of you as it has throughout your life.

"Whether you realize it or not, your unconscious mind has been taking care of you all along. For example, with your conscious mind you make a decision to cross the street. As you're crossing, your unconscious mind controls the muscles in your legs as you walk. Take tying your shoes as another example. You learn to tie them consciously, and now you probably tie them unconsciously, without thinking. I'm sure you trust yourself to tie your shoes without thinking, don't you?"

"Yes, but that's different," Loren answered. "I'm afraid of losing control. When I tie my shoes, I'm still able to decide what to do; I'm in control. But in hypnosis I might not be able to control anything."

At that point another member of the group, with whom I had worked previously, turned to Loren and said, "I think I know what you're saying. The first time Mac worked with me, I was scared too. But we agreed upon a signal—blinking my eyes—that I would use if things became uncomfortable. When I knew that I could stop the process, I felt in control. But I had to be willing to give up some conscious control, which was scary at first."

"You see," I said to the group, "it *is* important to be wary if you're overly susceptible to the suggestions and influence of other people, because hypnosis can be used manipulatively. However, I'm teaching you a process that you'll use by yourself. It requires that you have trust in yourself. The most important point I want to make about self-hypnosis is that eventually you'll be able to tap the power of your unconscious mind and make changes in your behavior."

The last question in the group session came from Loren. "Can you get stuck in an altered state," she asked, "and not be aware of danger, a fire, or an intruder?"

"My personal experience with self-hypnosis," I replied, "and the reported experiences of hundreds of others with whom I've worked, is that the unconscious mind is constantly and protectively monitoring the environment while you're in an altered state. When something very unusual occurs, you will be aroused from the trance state. As for getting stuck, I don't know anyone who stayed hypnotized longer than the time they set aside for it. It's possible, however, that you could fall asleep if your body needs rest. When that happens, the hypnotic state is erased."

Experiencing Self-hypnosis

If, after reading about the reactions to the Betty Erickson Technique, you feel comfortable and can see yourself doing it, then go back to page 128 and reread the steps in the process. Memorize them, and go to a quiet place where you won't be disturbed to experience the technique.

I encourage you to practice it every few days for several weeks until you can put yourself into an altered state within a few minutes. Each time you use it, decide on the amount of time you want to remain in an altered state so you can return to your normal activities when you want to. Your unconscious mind has its own timer, and I think you'll be surprised to find that you'll "come back" within a minute or two of the time you have established for yourself.

It's important to carefully monitor your state of consciousness *after* you return to the here-and-now. Determine exactly how long it takes you to return completely to your normal state of functioning. Most people come back to "normal" in a matter of moments; a few take up to an hour. It's possible to injure yourself if you engage in a potentially harmful activity before you're back to your normal state.

Applying Self-hypnosis

Self-hypnosis can be used in many ways to achieve worthwhile outcomes pertaining directly to golf or to your general well-being.

For General Well-Being and Health

An older, active, recreational athlete I knew used self-hypnosis to stop smoking cigarettes after smoking a pack a day for almost forty years. Smoking was interfering with his breathing when he played squash, and he knew it wasn't healthful.

Just before using self-hypnosis he instructed his unconscious mind to activate all the resources within himself that would make his heart and lungs function effectively, and to make his lungs clean and healthy. He also told his unconscious mind to do its work in its own way, in its own time. He followed the steps of the Betty Erickson Technique, remaining in an altered state for about twenty minutes.

He told me he didn't recall having any special images, memories, or sounds during that altered state. It was deep and relaxed. Nothing happened for about three weeks, and he continued to smoke. So he repeated the process.

A week or so later he woke up with a bad head cold. Because he didn't get much pleasure from smoking when he had a cold, his unconscious mind apparently chose that time to go to work. After several days of suffering from the miserable cold, he realized that he hadn't smoked for two days. He didn't deliberately stop; he just didn't smoke and wasn't aware that he had stopped, because he had no withdrawal symptoms. Almost ten years later he still doesn't smoke.

Several years ago I worked with an athlete who was an insomniac. She wanted to sleep six hours a night instead of her usual two or three. While in bed before going to sleep Sandy always reviewed in her mind what she wanted to do the next day. She'd worry so much about what had to be done the next day that she couldn't get to sleep.

During self-hypnosis an image of a piece of paper containing a list of chores flashed in her mind. From that image she decided to make a list of all the things she wanted to do *before* she went to bed. By making a list *before* bedtime she was more relaxed and overcame her insomnia.

Improving Athletic Skills

I also recall a high jumper who wasn't jumping as well as he had been. He experimented with modifying several parts of his performance, but without success. He decided to try self-hypnosis, instructing his unconscious mind to attend to the task of improving his jumping. During one session he had the image of a space shuttle blasting off from Cape Kennedy. He interpreted this image to mean he should apply more energy during his takeoff. It was something he hadn't thought of during his experiments. So at his next practice session he created that metaphorical image of the space shuttle at the time of takeoff, and he soared over the bar with an inch or two to spare.

There are several ways to improve your golf through self-hypnosis. One way is to give yourself the suggestion beforehand to experience fully a particular problem you are having with a certain kind of shot, followed by an experience that is exactly the opposite—when you were hitting that shot well. Then put yourself into an altered state and learn how to correct your swing from the images that are unconsciously produced. After "coming back" from an altered state, compare the images of the good and bad shots, looking for ways to correct your swing—sort of like the Get-It-Back Process and Discovering Difference.

Using self-hypnosis in a rather unusual way Bill Adams conquered a common problem—constantly comparing his score with par. When he did this, he became tense and didn't enjoy his game. He just wanted to have some fun while playing. This is how he used self-hypnosis.

He induced an altered state—a very light trance—and then actually hit tee shots and approach shots on the practice tee, while at the same time he was playing in his mind the first nine holes on the course.

Bill began to visualize the first hole, deciding where he wanted to place his drive; and then smacked the ball. The trajectory told him how close his shot matched what he'd imagined, whether he was in the fairway or rough, and how close he was to the flag. When he reached the green in his imagination, he mentally putted and finished the hole. While still on the practice ground he repeated the process for the remaining eight holes.

When he finished the "front nine" in his mind, I asked him if he'd shot par. Interestingly, he told me that he'd never thought about his score until that moment. He paused and then said he was one over, and then added, "That's the way I'd like to play all the time."

Bill walked from the practice tee to the putting green and then reversed the procedure for the "back nine." Here he mentally played all the shots from tee to green, imagining how far his mind shots were from the pin. He dropped a ball on the putting green in a position that corresponded to the imagined approaches. Then he putted the ball for real. I watched him two-putt every hole.

Since playing that trance round Bill told me he was playing his normal rounds in a much more relaxed state and paying less attention to his score.

Using Television

There's another way to use self-hypnosis as a means of improving your golf game. Billy Casper, a senior touring pro, uses it when he watches videotapes of his own performance.

I also have a technique for watching videotape recordings of either yourself, or professional golfers, making a good shot, after you've put yourself into an altered state.

Many pro shops at both private and public courses have videotapes of fine golfers for sale or rent at reasonable rates. Pros also make video recordings of their students for a nominal fee. It's also possible to have continuous replays of one or more golf swings reproduced on one videotape. The cost varies from one area of the country to another, but it can be done in a week's time for under a hundred dollars.

Here are the steps to follow if you want to view videotapes of yourself or other golfers while in an altered state. The idea is to refine and groove your setup and swing for a variety of shots while in an altered state. This is done through stimulating your unconscious neuromuscular swing mechanisms, capitalizing on the synesthesia patterns operating in your brain.

VIDEO OBSERVATION

1. Select the videotape of a pro golfer, or yourself, making a shot you want to mimic.
2. Give yourself the general suggestion to focus only on the central elements of the setup and swing of the shot you're about to observe.
3. Put yourself into an altered state. When ready, turn on the VCR with the sound off. While watching put yourself into the picture and feel in your muscles the mechanics of the setup and swing.

4. When finished allow yourself to come back to your "normal" state.
5. If convenient go to the practice tee or putting green to reproduce the video images as closely as possible. You may use the Get-It or the Get-It-Back Process, whichever is appropriate.

Here is a summary of the steps to follow when using self-hypnosis to improve your game.

ACHIEVING OUTCOMES WITH SELF-HYPNOSIS

1. Carefully specify what you want to accomplish.
2. Ask your unconscious mind to uncover all of the appropriate abilities and emotional states that will be needed to achieve the outcome, and to apply them when it's most appropriate.
3. Put yourself into an altered state, being curious about whether or not your unconscious mind will communicate in the form of spontaneous images, sounds, and feelings. Note what transpires and analyze their meaning *after* you come out of the altered state.
4. Interpret any images, sounds, and feelings as being *possible* ways to achieve your outcome. Put those ways into action and evaluate their effectiveness.

5. If you have no direct communication in the form of sights, sounds, and feelings from your unconscious mind during the altered state, do nothing deliberately to achieve your outcome. Trust your unconscious mind to do its work. Wait for several weeks. If you still haven't achieved your outcome, repeat the entire process.

TEN

Mind and Body: Generating Energy, Controlling Pain, and Hastening Healing

Golf is a safe and civil sport, but not always. In 1975 at a public course in suburban Washington, D.C., a golfing joust took place on one of the early holes. The second group claimed the first was holding it back; the first insisted the second hit into it. Carts sped at each other, their occupants waving clubs. Among the injuries was a fractured skull.

In a court in Inglewood, California, a man was convicted of beating and choking an opponent during a dispute over where a ball should have been placed on the green. A local rule in Uganda read, "If a ball comes to rest in dangerous proximity to a crocodile, another ball may be dropped." In Texas, Moody Weaver used such force during a swing that he broke his leg in two places, above the knee and above the ankle.

My techniques for generating energy, controlling pain, and getting healed more quickly are not limited to golfing Lancelots, or even golfers.

They are based on the principle that the mind affects the internal working of all the organs and systems of the body. Although we have very little hard scientific data that verify this principle, many physicians and other health specialists support it.

I know from my clinical experience, as do other medical and mental-health specialists, that the mind is a fantastic energizer. I know it acts like a powerful anesthetic, and it heals without chemical supplements or scalpels.

It is evident in the experience of those who undergo chest and abdominal surgery with self-hypnosis and *without* anesthesia; it is clear through the work of faith healers, shamans, and Indian medicine men; and it has been demonstrated by hundreds of people who cure themselves of all sorts of diseases.

All I ask is that you experience doing the techniques. Find out what happens when you use them. The absolute worst that can happen, if they work, is that you'll no longer have excuses for not playing well.

Before you use these techniques, however, **I encourage you to consult with your physician if you are run down and out of shape, have unexplained pain or physical symptoms, or are emotionally upset.** My techniques are meant to complement the work of health specialists, not to replace their services.

Energy Regulation

The spirit and physical capacity of the human being to accomplish extraordinary tasks in the face of utter fatigue is amazing. War veterans know only too well the meaning of carrying on with little or no sleep for days on end. As a coach I observed firsthand almost unbelievable performances by my swimmers during grueling practice sessions.

I know we can tap into our past memories of having

overcome fatigue as a way to deal with present tiredness. Consequently, I developed one simple anchoring technique that has proven to be effective in overcoming fatigue and maintaining a high-energy state for a short period of time.

Energy Anchor

The essence of the Energy Anchor is to remember a time when you overcame intense fatigue in the past—seeing, hearing, and feeling again, in specific detail, what you saw, heard, and felt then. Consider the following kinds of past experiences: (1) after a tedious day at work you engaged in an enjoyable physical activity and then felt renewed; (2) after a hard stint of labor that left you exhausted, you realized that with one last, big push you could finish the task at hand; and when you finished, you felt a sense of relief, satisfaction, and restored vigor; (3) having taken a break from a laborious task you returned to it enlivened; (4) you felt renewed and excited upon hearing a piece of good news.

After you access a renewed-energy experience, anchor the vigorous feeling when it's at its most intense level. Anchor it with a single image of that past experience, a sound that occurred then, or with some natural physical gesture. Practice firing the anchor three or four times a day for a week or two until the anchor is thoroughly established. In the future, when fatigue sets in and you want to feel restored, fire the anchor.

Energy Visualization

Energy can be produced by visualizing metaphorically the processes that are necessary to bring the body from a fatigued state to a vigorous one. Without going into the details of physiology the visualization consists of imagining: (1) the distribution of oxygen, stored chemicals, and nutriments to the muscles, (2) the chemical activity that occurs within muscle cells, and (3) the elimination of waste products from the body.

The following is a metaphor of the activity of the human body that a number of athletes have found useful to maintain their energy levels, as in running long-distance races.

As if from a point up in space they watch tankers (red blood cells) pick up oxygen gas from two storage depots (the lungs); seeing this they feel their bodies becoming lighter as they breathe in. They watch the tankers travel upriver (the bloodstream) to a factory in which there is a storage tank (nutriments) and a central workroom full of machines (the muscles). They watch the tankers unload the oxygen where it combines with the stored nutriments to become fuel for the muscles.

As the fuel is fed to the factory machines (the muscles), they see the levers working faster and smoother; while watching *this* they imagine their muscles working more energetically. They also see smoke (expired air) coming out of the factory chimney and imagine getting rid of waste products from their body as they exhale.

Whenever you feel sluggish on the golf course—when your swing lacks zip or your play is lethargic—just run the tanker movie in your mind, feel yourself becoming lighter as you inhale, feel more energetic while you swing, and, finally, imagine that you're blowing away the tiredness when you exhale. This metaphor is effective because it combines pictures of internal bodily activity with attention to breathing. One of the quickest ways to change your state of consciousness is to change your breathing—to increase its depth and to slow down its rate.

Kristin Larkin, one of my graduate students at Columbia University and a personal fitness trainer in New York City, developed a rather interesting metaphorical movie for maintaining her energy level during workouts. The elements of her metaphor parallel the physiological action that goes on in active muscle cells. She uses the movie in her mind while doing heavy exercise. After practicing it several times while working out, she noticed that her energy increased; as a result she gained more confidence in the worth of the visualization process.

This is her metaphor:

> I see a picture of myself working out on a television screen in front of me [a meta picture]. Superimposed on that picture is another picture of a large muscle cell.
>
> As I watch the cell ignite into an orange flame (chemicals in the cell combine to create energy), the larger picture of myself is changing. I see many pockets of flame multiply first in my legs and then spread to all parts of my body. As my workout gets heavier, I see millions of flaming cells igniting. I also see my legs puffing up with energy, and the image of myself becomes superwoman.
>
> As I watch myself working I notice a milky white substance (a buffering agent) mix with streams of yellow fluid (lactic acid) flowing from the flaming cells; this causes the yellow to fade away. Throughout the metaphor I imagine that I have more energy.

Kristin and I developed another metaphor which she uses for aerobics. She also recounts it to clients in her fitness classes. This metaphor is one that takes her back to her childhood. The idea of the metaphor is to get her to work *smoothly, strongly,* and in a *balanced* way when she's faced with increased activity. It involves eating fudge.

If you're a chocolate freak or have a weight problem, you might want to skip this one. If you decide to read on, eat fudge, and gain weight, you can blame it all on me.

> When I was a little girl, my mother used to make fudge and shared it with a neighbor. I'd be outside playing and I could smell that fudge. I'd go inside and watch her stir it until it got creamy, smooth, and thick. Then she'd pour it into a big pan. After waiting until it hardened she'd cut it all up into nice bite sizes so some of it could be delivered to a neighbor.
>
> Then I'd get on my bike with the fudge in my basket. As I pedaled up the hill to our neighbor's house, I could still smell the fudge. I looked forward to getting a piece of it when I got there.

Kristin interprets the metaphor in this way. The fudge represents her muscles—smooth, relaxed, and warm—being exercised (in riding up the hill on her bike, which required balance and strength). The memory of her mother's fudge motivates her to work out in a smooth, relaxed, and balanced way. The good feeling of taking a gift to a neighbor generates a just-right state for her.

Pain Control

When pain is present, the appropriate action is to consult medical specialists to identify its causes and provide appropriate treatment and medication. You can learn how to reduce it while still undergoing medical treatment. Let's consider three pain-reducing techniques.

Inside Out

Inside Out is a technique that effectively reduces pain resulting from emotional stress, injury, or surgery. I've used it with hundreds of people. It's a very simple six-step process, as illustrated by the work I did with Gail, who complained of having a severe headache with no apparent cause.

"On a scale from zero to ten," I said, "rate the severity of the pain that you're experiencing right now."

"It's a doozy," she replied. "Ten!"

"What I want you to do," I instructed her, "is to imagine what that pain looks like. Describe it to me as if you were looking at it on the wall over there. In fact, project the image of your pain on the wall and tell me precisely what it looks like."

"What it looks like?" she asked, looking puzzled.

"Sure. Tell me its shape and how big it is."

Gail paused, stared at the wall, and then said, "It's shaped like a small football. It's expanding and contracting, as if it were being squeezed. That's the way it feels here in the back of my head."

"Fine description," I said. "Tell me about its color, texture, and density."

"It's glowing red. It's really heavy and seems to be filled with thick pieces of rubber. It's very smooth, like plastic."

"Can you see that smooth, pulsating, glowing red football filled with rubber, on the wall right now?"

Gail nodded as her eyes focused and defocused on the wall.

"Hold that image there while doing something that may sound strange to you," I said. "Make a sound, either out loud or privately to yourself, that exactly matches the way your headache feels. Open your throat and let that feeling of pain come out!"

Gail's eyes defocused as she uttered a rather feeble "Ow."

"Open your throat, Gail, and let that sound come out freely and strongly," I told her.

This time Gail wailed loudly, "Oooowwww!"

"That's right. Keep your throat open and adjust the sound so that it matches your pain."

After listening to her wail for about ten seconds, I interrupted her, saying, "Stop the sound for a few seconds. In your peripheral vision project another image on the wall, an image of a place of pleasure where you've been in the past. Put that picture on the right edge of your vision, and keep the football image of your pain in the center."

"Okay, I've got the two pictures," she said.

I told her to start making the sound that matched her pain again, and to keep it going. Then I instructed her to imagine a wind blowing from right to left across her pictures. "Let the image of the pain vaporize and be blown away by the wind," I said, "as the picture of your place of pleasure moves to the center of your vision."

After about a minute Gail seemed to relax. Her posture slumped as her mouth opened and her chin dropped. "On a scale of zero to ten what's the intensity of your pain now?"

She paused for a few seconds and then said, "Two. The headache's almost gone. That's amazing. Can I use that process for other headaches and other pains?"

I told her it can be used for any kind of pain anytime, but she should check out her headaches and other persistent pains with her doctor.

INSIDE OUT

1. Identify the precise location of your pain and rate its severity on a scale from zero to ten.

2. Project a clear image of the pain on a nearby surface. Identify its size, shape, density, weight, thickness, surface texture, and color.

3. Holding that image in view, make a sound that matches its intensity. The sound should express exactly how the pain feels. If it's inconvenient to utter the sound aloud, "hear" it loud and clear in your mind. Vary its pitch, tone, and volume until it matches the feeling and intensity of your pain.
4. In your peripheral vision to the right, project an image of a remembered place of pleasure.
5. Again focus on the projected image of pain, express what it feels like vocally or silently, and pretend that the pain image is vaporizing. As it disappears, gradually lower the sound and let the image of the place of pleasure move to the center of your vision.
6. Rate the severity of pain that remains on a scale from zero to ten. Compare it with the original rating in Step 1.

The Inside Out technique usually reduces pain considerably, or eliminates it altogether. Metaphorically, you move the pain from inside your body to the outside; thus the title "Inside Out." The technique can be used almost anytime, and it's especially useful during a round of golf. Just project an image of your pain on a tree trunk, water cooler, or on an imaginary screen, following the instructions above.

"Swish"

"Swish," previously described on page 86, can also be used to reduce or eliminate pain. An image of the painful state can be the large projected image that is used in the "swish" process; it should be one color. A very small image representing the healed or painless state should be created and projected on top of the large image of pain at the seven-o'clock position. The smaller, second image should be another color.

To complete the "swish" process shrink the larger image until it fades away; at the same time increase the size of the small image until it's the only one remaining. Quickly repeat the "swish" process five times, letting your mind go blank after each "swish."

Self-hypnosis

I learned a process of alleviating pain with self-hypnosis from a twelve-year-old girl who suffered from sickle-cell anemia. It consists of imagining a dial with a control knob located on your mental screen. The dial indicates the intensity of a particular pain that you may have in a specific part of your body. The knob is used to regulate the intensity of the pain on the dial. As the needle on the dial registers the degree of pain, silently make a sound or tone that corresponds to the way the pain feels.

While in an altered state see an imaginary strand of nerves connecting the painful area of your body to the dial. Experiment with regulating the intensity of the pain. Increase it by turning the knob under the dial in one direction; decrease it by turning the knob in the opposite direction. As the needle registers a higher intensity of pain, feel the pain increase and hear the sound become louder. Then turn the knob in the opposite direction to reduce the pain and volume of sound as much as possible. Bring yourself back from the altered state to "normal." The pain should be entirely eliminated or reduced to a tolerable level.

If you have various kinds of pain in different parts of your body, you can create a console of dials, with each dial representing a specific pain. If you have more than one kind of pain, you can manipulate the appropriate dial for each pain.

Healing

During the last eight to ten years there have been many books written for laymen that focus on the mind-body relationship, especially as it relates to illness and healing. You might find some of them of particular interest: *Anatomy of an Illness* by Norman Cousins; *Getting Well Again* by Carl Simonton, a cancer specialist, and his associates; *Love, Medicine & Miracles* by Bernie Siegel, a surgeon; and *Minding the Body, Mending the Mind* by Joan Borysenko, director of the Mind/Body Clinic at Harvard Medical School. A more technical book that explains the theory behind mental healing is *The Psychobiology of Mind-Body Healing* by Ernest Rossi, a protégé of Dr. Milton Erickson.

Norman Cousins clearly demonstrates the power of his natural healing resources. With his doctor's medical expertise and encouragement and through humorous movies, books, and cartoons, he overcame his depression and disease. Laughter, and the positive emotional state which it evoked, proved to be an important part of his cure.

Bernie Siegel and Carl Simonton have demonstrated the power of the mind as an adjunct to medical treatment for cancer patients. Joan Borysenko describes an extensive preventative medicine program of mental/emotional techniques to supplement medical treatment at Harvard.

According to respected scientists we are able to heal ourselves by using mental processes. Simply stated, they believe that our thoughts and emotions affect body chemistry, especially hormones and neuropeptides. These chemicals affect our immune response to disease.

The essential elements of mental healing are a belief in

your own power to heal yourself and your ability to accurately visualize the physiological healing processes that help the body repair itself with or without the use of medicine and surgery.

Here are some examples of how several of my clients hastened their healing with metaskills techniques.

Torn Ankle Ligaments

Cynthia, a young figure skater who had orthopedic surgery for a serious foot injury, enhanced her recovery by her own unusual visualization process. She "saw" boatloads of little men in white hospital gowns traveling through her bloodstream to the site of the injury. They unloaded special ligament-stretching paraphernalia, sewing machines, and chemical nutriments. They then stretched the ligaments, sewed them securely to the bones in her foot, and sprinkled medicine on top of the ligaments.

She visualized another crew of garbagemen who cleaned up the waste left by her interior tailors and by the body's natural healing; they loaded the waste onto scows, which were dispersed through her blood vessels to her liver, kidneys, intestines, and lungs for eventual disposal outside of her body.

Cynthia held her own matinee movies every day during recovery. When she left the hospital her doctor told her that she had recovered from the surgery in an amazingly short period of time.

Hay Fever

Another athlete created an internal movie to eliminate sneezing during the hay-fever season. He imagines a team of men in white coats swabbing his sinus cavities with mops. Another team of men follows the first team and paints his sinus cavities with a molasses-type substance to prevent the infiltration of pollen and other irritating pollutants. The result: he stops sneezing and his nasal passages clear up.

Knee Surgery

Here's a personal testimony. In the early 1970s I had surgery on my left knee for a torn ligament. Ten years later I had severe pain and limited movement in my right knee. The orthopedic surgeon who had diagnosed and assisted in the left-knee surgery told me the same problem existed in my right knee. He prescribed surgery identical to the previous procedure.

I told him I wanted to use visualization to heal my knee before I underwent any surgery. I asked him to fully describe what had to happen for my knee to heal naturally. Although he was extremely skeptical, he told me what would have to happen inside the knee capsule. I left his office and he wished me success.

I created a metaphorical movie to parallel the healing and watched it in my mind daily for a couple of weeks and then once a week for several months. It is now seven years later and I no longer have pain. I had no surgery, and I'm as active as I was before my right knee acted up. I attribute this to my healing movie.

Below is a description of a simple visualization method of mental healing that I have developed and used successfully with scores of athletes; it doesn't always work. It's based primarily on Carl Simonton's work. You, too, can use it as a supplement to the treatment and medication prescribed by your physician. It consists of the following steps:

METASKILLS HEALING

1. Consult your physician and ask him to give you a complete and accurate description, in mechanical and chemical terms, of what must happen in your body to bring it back to normal, including the effects of medication on the healing processes. Make sure that you understand exactly what that process is by restating to your doctor in your own words his or her description. When the doctor verifies your layman's description, it becomes the basis for creating your own mental-healing movie.
2. Create a movie that metaphorically represents the mechanical and chemical processes of healing. (For example, a balloon deflating could represent reduction in swelling; a weaver working on a loom could signify the rejoining of torn tissue.)
3. "Run" your movie several times a day. Include a segment in the movie that portrays yourself as gradually healing, regaining energy, and becoming physically active again.
4. After successful healing, praise yourself for the work you've done.

If your condition doesn't improve following a week or so of visualization, then the process you've been using may need to be continued for several more weeks, or it may need to be changed. The ineffectiveness of your metaphorical movie could be the result of incomplete medical knowledge, since physicians are not always totally sure of exactly how medications work or precisely how the body heals. Therefore the movie may not represent the recovery process accurately. It's also likely that your movie may not match the doctor's description.

In any case your unconscious mind will indicate where the movie is inaccurate by distorted images, muffled sounds, and uncomfortable feelings as you watch. Corrections, based on more knowledge from your doctor and better interpretation of that knowledge on your part, can be made in the movie at the places where you experience distorted sensory information.

If your health status has not improved after changing the movie and watching it for several more weeks, then it makes sense to abandon the process and maybe see another doctor.

ELEVEN

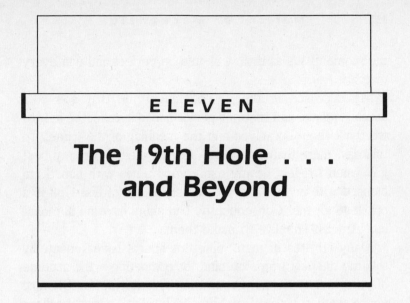

The 19th Hole . . . and Beyond

What you do with your mind off the golf course, without a club in your hand, is equally as important as applying metaskills techniques on the course to improve your swing and lower your handicap. So let's move to the 19th hole, where we can discuss a few things: what your outcomes and expectations might be, which metaskills techniques are most appropriate for getting what you want in golf, and making sure that you don't play mind games that keep you from enjoying golf and playing it well.

Expectations

Just how realistic are you about your golf game? When you miss the fairway, dub a shot, come up short of the green, or miss a birdie putt, are you upset? As I watch a lot of whimpering golfers trudge off a green, or see them pound their clubs into the ground with rage, it looks and sounds as though they expect a whole lot more than what is possible at the moment. It's as if they should be perfect and win every match.

My deceased brother, Ken, taught me that golf is a humbling game and that our performance is reflected in how we think about ourselves and the meaning of the game. To this day, more than ten years after he died, I play my best golf when I reflect on my many good times with him. I am blessed with my life and the remembrance of his. Golf is a privilege for me. Consequently, bad shots have no ill meaning. At least I'm alive to make them.

Many athletes in many different sports have repeatedly told me the best frame of mind for competing is the attitude of going out to have a good time. This is true for Olympic figure skaters, Grand Prix horseback riders, national-caliber fencers, racketball players, you name the sport.

Peter Jacobsen, after completing two mediocre rounds out of three in the 1988 U.S. Open, said to a *New York Times* reporter, "I felt like an old lawn mower that wouldn't turn over. I just couldn't get started. . . . After two 76's I said to myself this morning, 'What the heck, let's go out and have some fun,' and I felt real loose." Loose and fun, indeed. Peter recorded seven consecutive 3's on his card, made birdie putts on five of the first six holes, turned in a record-breaking score of 64, and went home with more than ten thousand dollars in prize money to boot. When fun, not score, is the desired outcome, then it doesn't matter what the score is; and more than likely the score will be a good one.

Be aware that ninety percent of tour golfers miss the fairway on the average of six out of eighteen holes; only ten percent of them can consistently hit twelve out of eighteen greens in regulation; and the very best of them break par only twenty-one to twenty-five percent of the time. And those people play golf and practice just about every day of the week practically all year long.

Pressure

Do you feel under pressure to shoot a lower score? If you do, don't tell me it's pressure put on by competitors, or spectators, or the media, or family and friends. It's certainly a fact that some sportscasters think that any exceptional tour golfer who doesn't win a tour championship has a "monkey on his back." That is, they *think* that the golfer feels pressure to win and can't because of the common expectation in our society that he *should* win. In actuality they are projecting what they themselves might feel if they were in the golfer's shoes.

The fact of the matter is that you, and only you, generate the pressure you feel. You put the monkey on your own back by accepting the common value of having to win. In effect you let yourself become brainwashed. You don't *have* to win.

Let's consider a simple example to illustrate what I mean. A two-foot putt is routine when you practice, but it can become a "pressure putt" and turn into a bogey on the 18th hole when you're one up. How is that pressure generated? From inside of you by virtue of how you think. It could spring from a number of thoughts—your desire, if not compulsion, to shoot a lower score and feel satisfied, to please someone else, to get recognition, or just to win. If winning or doing well aren't important, then making the putt doesn't matter; the pressure is removed.

Winning

Many golfers heap enormous pressure on themselves to win. Having to win, feeling *compelled* to win, is bad because it generates muscle tension that interferes with making a smooth swing. *Wanting* to win out of genuine desire, on the other hand, serves as motivation to excel. When you excel, you give your opponents something to shoot at. I don't know anybody who wants to compete with someone who doesn't give a damn about winning.

I strongly believe that the better my opponent plays, the more opportunity I have to challenge myself and dig deeper into my resources. In this way I really challenge my opponent. The better each of us plays, the better each of us can become. When a golf match is approached with this perspective, opponents become fellow players who appreciate each other; they aren't simply objects to be defeated.

In my associations with fine athletes in many sports, nearly all of them say that when they play their best against top-flight opponents, victory becomes a highly prized bonus—a bonus because of the satisfaction of reaching a personal-best performance goal. Even if they lose under the same circumstances, they have a bittersweet feeling—disappointment with the loss coupled with the satisfaction of playing well. In contrast they say that a victory that comes after playing poorly, irrespective of the opponent's quality of play, provides very little satisfaction.

The saving grace of golf is its handicap system. We can truly challenge our opponents to play well despite our differences in ability. At the same time we can challenge ourselves to play equal to or better than our own handicap.

If you find that you're pressuring yourself to win, it might be important to ask yourself what would happen if you didn't win. What would you lose besides the match? Would you feel as if you were letting someone else down—your pro, your playing partner, your family or friends? Would you feel bad by letting them down?

If the answer is yes, it's quite likely that you're taking

unrealistic responsibility for how others feel, and getting your own sense of satisfaction from them instead of from yourself. This means that you're unnecessarily dependent upon others for feeling good about how you play. You're playing a dependent "mind game" instead of taking full responsibility for your own actions and feelings. In other words you're operating in your mind as if you were out there for someone else.

You don't play golf, or do anything else for that matter, for another person. *Everything you do is for yourself.* Even when you do something to please someone else, you do it because you get something in return—enjoyment from playing the game, love, recognition, money, whatever—or you do what you do to avoid something such as criticism or punishment.

What else might happen if you didn't win? Would you feel embarrassed? Would you feel inadequate as a person? Would you feel dissatisfied with yourself? If your answer to these questions is yes, then your chances of feeling good about yourself are dim, since only one player wins a tournament; the rest lose. Unfortunately, the we're-number-one mania in the sports world is another "mind game" that feeds an irrational sense of the value of a scoreboard victory.

The true measure of the worth of your golf game and yourself is how you feel about your own efforts. If you believe you really applied yourself, irrespective of your score, that's all that anyone can ask. It's natural to feel disappointment with poor play. Embarrassment, however, implies a low sense of self-esteem, because you allow those who watch you to determine your self-worth.

So striving to win creates a paradox. If you try too hard, if you're compelled to win, you'll generate pressure that results in poor play; if you leave winning aside and tell yourself to just enjoy playing, as Peter Jacobsen did, it's highly likely that you'll play well. It also means you have a better chance to win. When you enjoy yourself and incidentally win, it feeds your sense of accomplishment, satisfaction, and self-worth.

"Shouldniks"

It's easy to spot dependent, compulsive people who put tremendous pressure on themselves to win or play perfectly. Just listen to their language. They use phrases containing "need to," "must," "got to," "have to," or "should"—"I've *got to* practice my long irons"; "I *should* be on the green in two"; "I *should* have made a par"; "I *need to* make that putt"; or "I've *got to* follow through on my sand shots." When examined carefully I'd bet that most bogeys, double bogeys, and missed birdie putts arise from being what I call a "shouldnik."

There's a very simple way to eliminate the internal mind game that creates such pressure. It merely involves substituting the phrase, "I *want* to do X because . . ." for the words "I *must* or *should* do X." When you say "want" with conviction, followed by a reason, you take full responsibility for your wishes and actions. As a result you'll either release a source of energy and motivation to accomplish X, or you'll realize that you're incapable of doing X, or don't want to do it at all.

Here's an assignment. Make sure you follow it exactly! If you already feel pressure to comply with my command, you'll know that you have a tendency to be a "shouldnik," and this exercise may help you overcome this tendency. For two weeks I encourage you to become acutely aware of every time you say, "I should," or its equivalent. When you consciously hear it, pay careful attention to how you feel inside—your bodily sensations—just after you admonish yourself. Then substitute the phrase "want" for "should" and pay attention again to the physical sensations in your body. Compare the two and notice the difference.

Do an exercise with me now. Say to yourself with conviction, "I should . . ." (insert something you've been putting off, such as practicing sand shots, working on your short game, cutting the grass, balancing the checkbook, washing windows, writing to so and so). What does it feel like in your body when you say this? Make a mental note of the physical feelings.

Now say to yourself, "I *want* to . . ." (insert what you said you *should* do), paying close attention to the bodily sensations that are generated as you think about doing it. Are the "want" feelings different from the "should" feelings? Do you still want to do it? Are you more determined than before to do it? Do you want to get someone else to do it for you? Or do you want to scrap the whole idea?

I can almost guarantee that if you use this exercise faithfully for two full weeks—substituting "want" for every time you say "should"—you'll feel much differently about yourself and your life. If you feel that you *should* complete this assignment, ask yourself if you really want to. It's important that you do it out of desire, not compulsion.

Perfectionism

Frequently, "shouldniks" are perfectionists. Perfectionists are people who leave no stone unturned to make whatever they do absolutely perfect, without flaw. They are relentless. Please don't misunderstand me. Doing things superbly and paying attention to detail is very important. Perfectionism, though, is the compulsion that things *must* be just so; it generates a pressure to perform beyond anyone's capability, let alone your own.

There is no such thing as a perfect golf shot. "Perfect"

performance in golf, as in any sport, is a paradox. A truly fine golf shot actually evolves out of exquisite ongoing, unconscious correction of error. You make the necessary modifications in your swing automatically when what you're actually doing doesn't match your intention. The better the golfer, the more corrections he makes. He's a master at making unconscious corrections. When you accept this, perfection becomes a myth. Perfection is replaced with the knowledge that making errors and correcting them is what makes a good golf shot, including a hole-in-one.

Peter Famiano, the club pro at Crestmont, reframed his own dogged determination to play perfectly by accepting the concept of error correction. He gave himself permission to make mistakes on the golf course, since they were inevitable. He anchors this state by carrying a South African golf pencil in his pocket when he competes. South African pencils, unlike U.S. golf pencils, have erasers on them.

If you're a "shouldnik" or a perfectionist, hitting a poor shot is analogous to having an unplayable lie. Even though you might be able to hit the ball feebly, give yourself relief. In your mind move two club lengths away from compulsive perfection and take a free drop into a place of curiosity. On the course take a lesson, drop another ball (if you're not playing a match), and find out how to correct your errant shot.

Establishing Outcomes

Since you can't play perfectly, what is it that you want to achieve in golf? Part of the metaskills approach is to use a systematic way of deciding what's worth achieving—your outcomes—and how you can get them with various techniques. This is accomplished by following some basic principles.

Principle of Positivity

Whenever golfers come to me for help, my first question is "What do you want to accomplish?" Invariably, they begin by telling me what's the matter with their game and what they don't want. Since this approach is usually, but not always, self-defeating, I play a mind game with them. Let's try an experiment right now to illustrate a very important point that could make your golf game so much better with very little work.

In about ten seconds I'm going to tell you to do something. At that time pay attention to what you experience inside—what you see and hear in your mind and what you feel in your muscles and other parts of your body. Get ready to follow my instructions. . . . Here goes: Don't be aware of your breathing right now.

What happened inside? If you're a normal human being, you automatically paid attention to your breathing—perhaps you felt the rise and fall of your chest and the movement of your abdomen as you inhaled and exhaled. Perhaps you heard the sound of air in your nostrils. If not, check again to see if you're still alive. If so, how come you became aware of your breathing when I told you *not* to?

To understand my direction *not* to pay attention to your breathing, you *had* to turn your mind to the act of breathing. The reason you couldn't *not* become aware of your breathing is the fact that language, the nervous system, and muscles are "wired" together, but words like *not* and *don't* are totally ignored. In other words the nervous system knows no negation.

If you say to yourself, "Don't slice the ball into the woods," you will access, consciously or unconsciously, a memory of having hit a slice in the past. The neural pathways between your brain and the muscles that control slicing will be automatically activated also, probably without your being aware of it. Consequently, you'll more than likely slice the ball into the trees bordering the fairway.

Of course, you can block this by consciously rehearsing a straight shot down the middle of the fairway in your mind while taking a proper practice swing. There are many people who consistently process information, consciously or unconsciously, by bringing counterexamples—opposites—to mind. Some of those people first think about what they don't want—a slice—and then they shift automatically to thinking about what they do want—a straight shot. Others first think about how they want to hit the ball, yet unconsciously shift to thinking about what they don't want to hit. This form of unconscious thinking can be devastating to your golf game if you're not aware of it.

As you think about your golf game right now, consider what you want to be able to do. If you find yourself saying something like "I don't want to take so many shots getting out of bunkers," just turn it around and say, "I want to get out of sand traps easily with one stroke." Do you feel differently inside when you say this?

Principle of Specificity

The more you know precisely what you want to accomplish, the easier it will be to get. You could say, "I want to be able to draw and fade my shots consistently." That statement can be further specified to include a more precise definition of "consistently," such as hitting them eight out of ten times from the tee.

The statement can be refined still further by identifying, in sensory-specific terms, what you would see, hear, and feel as you execute those shots. For example, you might want to change your stance; you might want to modify the swing path of the club in the impact area; you might want to adjust your grip and lengthen or shorten your backswing; you might want to hear a certain kind of click when the club strikes the ball; or you might want to visualize a certain kind of trajectory.

Sometimes it's hard to pinpoint how your setup or swing could be changed to improve your game. This is especially true for low handicappers, because everything is so grooved. Frequently the clue to your corrections is reflected in language, especially the verbs, adverbs, and adjectives that are used to describe a swing problem.

Once while I was working with a golfer on the practice tee, she said to me, "My swing doesn't *feel harmonious.*" This statement suggested that there were both kinesthetic (feel) and auditory (harmonious) components to her swing analysis.

Then I asked her, "Which muscles specifically don't *feel* right and what kind of *sound* would you like to go along with your swing?"

After swinging her club a few times she replied, "Oh, now I know what it is. I don't feel the flexibility in my wrists and the ever-so-slight pause at the top of my backswing that I normally feel when I swing with rhythm. I'm not humming the phrase of a song in my mind as I usually do. Let me hum my tune and hit it again."

After hitting a few shots she said, "Now it feels the way I want it to."

My work with her was finished. I had just pointed her in the direction of her own knowledge. Metaskills techniques do exactly that.

The Backup Process

There's another way to uncover unknown elements of your game in need of refinement. It's called the Backup Process.

Essentially, it consists of mentally rehearsing your *anticipated* performance for a *forthcoming* tournament. During your mental review, defects in your performance will be revealed in the form of unclear images, garbled and discordant sounds, and uncomfortable feelings. These distorted sensory data are forms of communication from your unconscious mind about aspects of your game that need attention.

As a result of doing the Backup Process you'll uncover information about the specific parts of your game in need of strengthening. You may notice blurred images during pitch shots or long putts. They are signals that it may be important to spend more time on the practice green honing your pitching and putting skills. If you feel uncomfortable while playing certain holes, it could indicate the need to play those holes repeatedly to familiarize yourself with the hazards and the contour of the land. If your pictures are fuzzy as you address the ball, it could mean that your setup is defective.

THE BACKUP PROCESS

1. Go forward to a tournament or competitive round on a course with which you're familiar and play a mental round. Fantasize, in full sensory detail, the conditions you believe will be present.
2. See, hear, and feel all that you would expect to see, hear, and feel as you mentally play each hole. If any of these representations are incomplete, discordant, unclear, or uncomfortable during your fantasy, it's a signal from your unconscious mind about elements of your game in need of improvement.

3. After you have identified what needs to be worked on, *take a step backward.* Fantasize how you would prepare for that competition, knowing the weakness your mind has discovered.
4. Scoot to the practice range and work on what needs improvement.

Repeat the Backup Process periodically to identify other potential outcomes. When the mental rehearsal for the future is devoid of defective sensory data, you can feel reasonably confident that you're fully prepared for a future tournament.

Principle of Ecology

Everything with which human beings interact has a definite impact upon their well-being. There is an interdependence between our beliefs, behaviors, expectations, nutrition, health, personal relationships, and the environment. Change any one of these elements and it could have a powerful effect on each of the others.

One woman improved her golf game so much that her husband, who didn't play as well as she did, felt threatened and they became temporarily estranged. One young man discovered, in the process of refining his golf game, that he really didn't want to reach his goal of becoming a tour golfer. He realized it would not be stimulating enough intellectually and would take too much time away from his wife. As a result he revised his career goals and is training to become a lawyer.

Another golfer who made fundamental changes in his grip and swing found his entire golf game temporarily out of whack. Because he wasn't playing as well as before, his family life became strained. Conversely, a tour golfer who changed his perspective about how he trained made a dramatic improvement in his game. Instead of dedicating himself to grueling practice sessions he adopted a laid-back attitude. When he was training intensely, his earnings on the tour were almost nil. When he loosened up, he "came back" and won.

These examples demonstrate the importance of paying close attention to the ecology of our lives—the interdependence of our beliefs and behaviors and our environment—whenever we make changes in our behavior, even changes in the way we play golf.

You can determine the ecological soundness of any desired outcome by answering two sets of important questions:

- What will achieving a particular outcome do for you? What will be the outcomes of that outcome?
- What's the worst that could happen if you achieve your outcome? Can you think of any reason why achieving the outcome would *not* be in your best interests?

By answering these questions you will identify the potential positive and negative effects of achieving an outcome *before* you pursue it. By doing this you will either become more strongly motivated to achieve a desired outcome or realize that its achievement may not be worth the effort. In both cases you'll save time and energy and avoid potential disappointment and disruption in your life.

Here are the steps to follow to establish ecological outcomes. Knowing them you'll be ready to select the appropriate metaskills techniques to achieve them.

ESTABLISHING OUTCOMES

1. Identify a shot that you want to learn or improve. Do this by using the Backup Process to analyze your performance, or consult with your pro.
2. State your outcome in positive terms. Indicate what you want, not what you don't want (Principle of Positivity).
3. Identify and evaluate the potential positive and negative consequences of achieving an outcome *before* you pursue it. If your evaluation is positive, continue to the next step. If not, go back to step 1 and identify another outcome (Principle of Ecology).
4. Define your outcome in precise sensory terms, knowing what you will see, hear, and feel when your outcome has been achieved (Principle of Specificity).

Going for It

Like swinging a golf club, using your mind can be complicated. But the proven process of learning the golf swing can be applied to learning how to use your mind. Just pay attention to only one or two keys at a time until they become automatic. Work with only one metaskills technique at a time. Gradually, you'll learn to swing your mind and your moods so that you can swing the club better from the inside out.

But which metaskills techniques are most appropriate for

your specific outcomes? I have prepared an outline with page references in Appendix C. It describes briefly the purposes of each technique and which ones can be used to achieve various outcomes. It serves as a quick reference to help you select the technique most appropriate for the particular outcome you have in mind. Frequently, more than one technique can be used to achieve an outcome; and most techniques can be applied to achieve a number of different outcomes.

I suggest that you approach the use of my techniques in an experimental way. By that I mean, fully commit yourself to following the steps of each technique several times exactly as presented. While doing this notice what happens to your performance. When one technique doesn't work, use another.

After each practice session and each round of golf, ask yourself the question "What did I learn?" regardless of the results. I really want you to think deeply about what you learn about yourself—your moods, the way you think, the things you value, and the way you feel about life and golf. Then truly honor what you've discovered about your inner self. When you know and honor yourself, you can then do as Shivas Irons whispered to Michael Murphy in *Golf in the Kingdom:* "When ye swing, put all yer attention on the feelin' o' yer inner body—*yer inner body.*"*

Published by the Viking Press (New York, 1972); reprint Delta Books (New York: Dell Publishing, 1973).

Selected References: Neuro-Linguistic Programming

1. Andreas, Steve and Connirae. *Change Your Mind—And Keep the Change*. Moab, Utah: Real People Press, 1987.
2. Bandler, Richard. *Using Your Brain—For a Change.* Moab, Utah: Real People Press, 1985.
3. Bandler, Richard, *Magic in Action.* Cupertino, California: Meta Publications, 1984.
4. Bandler, Richard, and John Grinder. *Reframing: Neuro-Linguistic Programming and the Transformation of Meaning.* Moab, Utah: Real People Press, 1982.
5. Bandler, Richard, and John Grinder. *Frogs into Princes.* Moab, Utah: Real People Press, 1979.
6. Bandler, Richard, and John Grinder. *The Structure of Magic,* Vol. 1. Palo Alto: Science and Behavior Books, 1975.
7. Bandler, Richard, and Will MacDonald. *An Insider's Guide to Sub-modalities.* Cupertino, California: Meta Publications, 1988.
8. Cameron-Bandler, Leslie. *They Lived Happily Ever After.* Cupertino, California: Meta Publications, 1978.

9. Dilts, Robert B., et. al. *Neuro-Linguistic Programming,* Vol. 1. Cupertino, California: Meta Publications, 1980.
10. Grinder, John, and Richard Bandler. *The Structure of Magic,* Vol. 2. Palo Alto, California: Science and Behavior Books, 1976.
11. Laborde, Genie Z. *Influencing with Integrity: Management Skills for Communication and Negotiation.* Palo Alto, California: Science and Behavior Books, 1984.
12. McMaster, Michael, and John Grinder. *Precision: A New Approach to Communication.* Beverly Hills: Precision Models, 1980.
13. Robbins, Anthony. *Unlimited Power.* New York: Simon and Schuster, 1986.
14. Yeager, Joseph. *Thinking about Thinking with NLP.* Cupertino, California: Meta Publications, 1985.

APPENDIX A

Uptime Cues

The following list of "uptime" visual, kinesthetic, and auditory cues constitutes the sensory information that golfers have found useful in regulating their golf game *while* they set up and swing:

Visual

The golf ball itself.

Printing on the ball.

The back surface of the ball set on a tee.

Spot in front of ball that represents its projected path. The target, the flag, the hole, a spot on the fairway or green.

Alignment of club face with respect to the target and ball.

Alignment of club shaft with respect to the ball and parts of the body (e.g., shoulders, hips).

Path of club face during initial portion of take-away.

Path of club face in the impact area.

Position of hands in relation to the ball at time of impact.

Position of hands on the club.

Position of the shoulders in relation to the target.

Position of the sternum in relation to the ball.

Position of feet in relation to the ball.

Position of feet in relation to the target.

Position of the hips and abdomen at the finish of the swing.

Position of the club face at the end of a chip and putt.

Degree to which a lofted club is held in an open position.

Kinesthetic

"Seated" posture.

Knee flexion.

Straightness of back.

Softness of grip.

Tension of last three fingers of left hand on club.

Tension of middle two fingers of right hand on club.

Sensitivity to weight distribution at the address position.

Flexibility of wrists.

Sensitivity of fingers.

Steadiness of head.

Straight left arm during backswing and downswing.

Tension/relaxation of wrist and arm muscles.

Tension/relaxation of shoulders and neck.

Tension/relaxation of legs.

Degree of wrist flexion, if any, at the start of the take-away.

Turning of shoulders during the backswing.

Shifting of weight, if any, during the swing.

Flexion and extension of the wrists during swing.

Turning of the hips during downswing.

Speed of the clubhead during swing.

Impact of club face on the ball.

Impact of club face with turf while taking a divot.

Position of hands during the follow-through.

Extent of the "finish" of the swing.

Auditory

Sound of *whoosh* during swing.

Sound of club face striking the ball.

Sound of club face taking a divot.

Sound of club face brushing the grass.

Sound of exhalation at impact.

The following are additional "uptime" cues that guide the golfer in making decisions about a shot immediately at hand:

Visual

Lie of the ball.

The flagstick.

Distance of ball from flagstick.

Location of hazards between ball and green (e.g., trees, traps, rough).

Location of "casual water."

Distance of ball from hazards.

Out-of-bounds markers.

Tee markers.

Thickness of the grass.

Wetness of the turf.

Contour of surrounding land and its slope toward water.

Contour of the fairway, the land surrounding the green, and the green.

Color of the sand in the traps.

Movement of leaves in trees created by the wind.

Movement of flag created by the wind.

Location of the northerly direction.

Color of grass on the putting surface.

Location of the cup.

Debris on putting surface between ball and cup.

Ball marks on the green.

Cleat marks on the green.

Shadows on the green.

Identification marking on the clubhead.

Lightning.

Auditory

Wind in the trees.

Wind across ears.

Sound of cleats on the turf and sand.

Thunder.

Kinesthetic

Softness/hardness of turf or sand underfoot.

Movement of wind over skin.

Rain.

Pressure of grass on sole of club during practice swing in rough.

Ambient air temperature on the skin.

APPENDIX B

Sensory Awareness

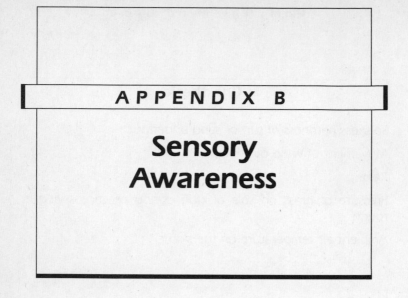

This appendix contains two parts: (1) a series of questions that identify how people internally represent their sensory experience; and (2) exercises designed to strengthen sensory awareness.

Representation of Sensory Experience

The questions that follow are a modification of what Richard Bandler and Will MacDonald presented in their book, *An Insider's Guide to Sub-modalities*. Submodalities are classified according to each of the three main channels of awareness that are crucial for regulating athletic skills, namely: vision, audition (sound), and kinesthesia (feeling). The senses of smell and taste are of little consequence in sports, except when fear is involved. Then both smell and taste seem to be quite important.

These questions are a handy reference when you're

practicing several metaskills techniques: Sherlock Holmes Exercise, Cross-over Training, Uptime Anchor, Just-right Anchors, Discovering Differences, Body Scanning, "Swish," and Self-hypnosis. Whenever any of the instructions for these techniques tell you to change *how* you see, hear, and feel "on the inside" or in your mind, the questions below can help you do just that.

Vision

Brightness—Are the images brighter than normal, with lots of light, or are they dark?

Color—Are images in color or only in black and white? Is there a full spectrum of color, or is there a dominance of one or more colors?

Contrast—Is there a sharp contrast in the objects and colors or are they subdued or washed out?

Focus—Are the images sharply focused or fuzzy?

Distance—Are you looking at the image as if zoomed in, or do you have a wide-angle view? How wide is the angle?

Location—Where is the image located in space? Is it within your head? Or is it located outside of you, to the front, side, rear, down, up? How far away is it (in feet and inches)? Does the screen on which the image is projected move? If so, in what direction?

Size—How big is the image (approximately, in inches or feet)? Does the size change?

Shape—Is the image round, square, triangular, rectangular?

Border—Does the image have a frame or border? Describe its size and design.

Viewpoint—Are you seeing yourself in the picture as if you were a spectator, or are you seeing what you would normally see if you were actually there in that place at that time? From what direction are you looking at yourself—from the side (right or left), back, front, above, at an angle? Is the image tilted at an angle from front to back or from side to side? Does the image seem to wrap around you, or is it flat or two-dimensional?

Motion—Is the image a still picture, or are you watching a movie? Are there a series of images like slides flashing on the screen one by one? Do you see multiple still pictures at the same time or all at once? If you're seeing a movie, is it like a film loop running over and over again? How fast are the motion pictures moving? Normal speed? Slower or faster than normal?

Number—How many images are there? Are they separate? Superimposed? Are they side by side or vertically arranged?

Audition (Hearing)

Volume—How loud is the sound? Is it normal? Above or below normal?

Duration—Does the sound persist, or is it intermittent?

Pitch—Are the sounds high or low pitched? Is the pitch higher or lower than normal?

Tone—Are the sounds thin? Full? Rich? Grating? Harsh? Pleasant? Resonant?

Melody—Is the sound harmonious? Discordant? A monotone?

Tempo—Is the beat fast or slow?

Rhythm—Is the beat syncopated of even-cadenced?

Location—Where is the source of the sound located? At a particular point within your body? Outside your body? Where, specifically, is the source of the sound located outside your body?

Direction—In what direction does the sound flow? Does it flow from inside out? Outside in? Upward? Downward? Is the sound stereophonic or do you hear it from only one direction?
Background—Are there background noises? If so, ask the above questions.

Kinesthesia (Feeling)

It's important to distinguish the feelings that signify an emotional state as contrasted with the feelings of skillful movement performance. Movement can be more or less skillful depending on the nature of the emotional state. Each of the categories below applies to both skillful performance and emotional states.
Location—Where, specifically, in your body do you feel the sensations? Does the feeling remain in one place or does it spread? Is the feeling localized, diffused, or the same throughout your body? Is there a difference in feelings on each side of your body? Is there a difference in feelings in the upper half as contrasted with the lower half of your body?
Duration—Do the feelings persist, or are they intermittent?
Characterization—How would you describe the quality of the feelings? Warm/cold? Relaxed/tense? Heavy/light? Extended/contracted? Even/pulsating? Strong/weak?
Movement—How would you describe the nature of your movements? Strong/weak? Coordinated/ disjointed? Gentle/ballistic? Smooth/jerky? Flexible/limited? Relaxed/tense? Slow/quick? Balanced/unbalanced?
Intensity—How strong are the sensations? What is the degree of strength, power, balance, relaxation, flexibility, smoothness, warmth, lightness, coordination, in relation to normal?

Sensory-Awareness Exercises

Few people process visual, auditory, and kinesthetic information equally well. Most of us are strong in the use of one or two sensory systems and weak in others. The exercises that follow are designed to strengthen your weaker senses. Most of the exercises can be done at any time, anywhere—while on the practice tee, riding to work, listening to a boring lecture, showering, cutting the grass, or waiting for the duffers ahead to clear out of range.

These exercises are merely examples of a few ways to improve your sensory awareness; use your ingenuity to create others.

Cross-over Training

Cross-over Training is a series of exercises that make use of the natural, inborn, synesthesia "wiring" in your brain and nervous system. They capitalize on the strength of your most sensitive sensory channel as a way to build up your sensitivity in other channels.

Cross Over from Hearing to Other Channels

Hear a bird sing and make a *picture* of a bird in your mind. *Hear* an automobile horn and *feel* the vibrations of the horn in some part of your body. In your mind *hear* the *click* of a past approach shot and *feel* the swing that put the ball within a tap-in distance of the cup.

Cross Over from Feeling to Other Channels

When you *feel* anger, see a color. Convert a painful *feeling* into the *sound* "Ouch!" While *feeling* the actual swing of your putter, generate in your mind's eye an *image* of a ball leaving the putter head, rolling toward the cup, and going into the hole.

Cross Over from Seeing to Other Channels

Make an internal *image* of a fire engine and *hear* its siren in your mind. Make a picture in your mind of a pleasant *scene* and pay attention to where in your body you have a pleasant *feeling*. *Observe* someone lifting something heavy and *feel* the strain of the muscular effort involved in your own muscles. Create an internal *image* of a golfer hitting a tee shot and *hear* in your mind the *click* of the club face on the ball. Remember the *trajectory* of a fine tee shot and *feel* the swing that produced it. *Watch* the roll of a superb putt and feel the *swing effort* that got the ball into the hole.

Watch the reflection of your setup and swing in a mirror or glass patio door, paying particular attention to various elements of the address and swing—the position of the club face, for instance, or the position of your hands and the club at the top of the backswing. When you *see* that the position in question is correct, pay attention to the *muscle feelings* associated with it. Close your eyes and reproduce those swing feelings several times. Open your eyes and check the swing in the mirror or glass door. Repeat this exercise until you're sure you have the muscle feelings of the proper swing without having to rely on the reflections.

Visual Imagery

Internal visual imagery is central to playing golf well. It prepares you mentally for each shot and helps you analyze and correct your golf swing. The exercises below are designed to increase your internal visual skills.

Making Meta Pictures

A meta picture is an internal image in which you see yourself as if you are looking through someone else's eyes, like watching yourself swing a club on videotape. This is an important imagery skill because it helps you evaluate your own golf swing.

- Seated comfortably in a chair, wiggle your toes and feel your feet on the floor. Now make a picture of only your feet. Next, move your lower leg and make a picture of it from the knee down; connect that picture to the one of your feet. Next, contract your thigh muscles, move your leg, and make a picture of your thigh; connect that picture to the previous picture of your lower legs and feet. Continue until you have connected all of you together. Don't forget your head. By this time you should have a complete meta picture of yourself.
- Practice making meta pictures of yourself while swinging a golf club. Become very sensitive to what each part of your body is doing throughout the swing—head, shoulders, arms, hands, torso, hips, legs, feet.
- Watch a portion of a videotaped recording of a pro's golf swing. Stop the tape, close your eyes, and visually reproduce the swing in your mind. Replay the videotape to determine the accuracy of your internal movie. Adjust

your internal images until they match the swing on the video screen.

Making Superimposed Pictures and Multiple Images

- Superimpose a tiny image of a flagstick onto a golf ball as you address it; in your mind make that picture bigger, as if you are using a zoom lens. Notice if you can see the ball for a longer period of time when you swing and hit it. What effect did this have on the quality of that shot?
- Project onto the surface of an actual green an imaginary moving picture of a golf ball rolling into the cup.
- On an imaginary screen located within your head, project four slide pictures of your swing; the slides consist of the take-away, the top of the back swing, the position of the club at impact, and the follow-through position. Use these mental slides as a guide for practicing your swing. Before setting up to a ball, generate the slide pictures in your mind and feel the swing. Then address the ball, let your mind go blank, turn, and swing. Does your swing improve?
- Make a movie of your swing in your mind's eye, and vary its brightness, sharpness, size, color, and focus. Notice what effect these variations have on your swing.

Auditory Awareness

I'm sure you realize that there are times on the golf course when you talk to yourself or hear the voices of others in your mind telling you what to do or what not to do. They can be useful when they're in your control or a hindrance when they're not. Similarly, external noises can be distracting when making a golf shot unless you know how to tune them out or use them constructively. Below are exercises to increase your sensitivity to sounds and make use of them in your mind to make your golf game better.

External Auditory

- Listen to the voice of someone on radio or television; turn off the sound and mimic the tone, volume, and syntax of the voice; turn the sound back on and compare the sound of your own voice with the one you heard. Repeat this process until you can mimic the voice as well as possible.
- Mimic as well as you can the sounds of animals as you hear them—a bird singing, for example, or a dog barking.
- Listen intently to a distracting sound while striking a golf ball. Notice the quality of the shot. Now pretend the distracting sound is entering your muscles, creating energy in your body and making your swing more powerful. Notice the quality of the shot. Is there a difference?
- Listen intently to a distracting sound as you are preparing to make a shot. Immediately shift your attention to peering at one dimple on the golf ball. Make the shot as you focus intently on the dimple. Notice the quality of the shot. Reflect on what happened to the distracting sound.

Internal Auditory

- Modify the volume and tone of your own or someone else's voice that you hear inside your head. Vary the nature of the internal voice from loud, harsh, and critical to soft, pleasant, and supportive. Notice how your bodily sensations vary with the change in tone and volume.

- When you hear an internal critical voice, substitute pleasant music. Notice any change in physical tension.
- Deliberately talk to yourself *while* teeing off and notice the quality of the shot. Then quiet your mind, hit another ball, and notice the quality of that shot. Is there a difference?
- Immediately after making a poor shot, deliberately criticize yourself harshly in your mind and notice the amount of tension in your body. Then stop criticizing yourself and without further thought drop another ball, swing, and notice the quality of that shot. Is the second shot better or worse than the first? If better, perhaps you were too tense on the first shot; if worse, perhaps you became too relaxed.
- Now change the internal critical voice to a calm, supportive one, giving yourself positive instructions about making a good swing. How much physical tension do you feel when you change your internal voice from being critical to supportive?

Kinesthetic Awareness

Contrary to logical expectation, I have found that many athletes are largely unaware of their bodily sensations. Golfers in particular are insensitive to the specific muscle tensions involved in hitting a golf ball, and they are unaware of the bodily sensations that are linked to their emotional states when they are swinging a club. Lacking these sensitivities, golfers are missing important information that could improve their game immensely. For example, if you're unaware of the amount of tension in your hands, wrists, and forearms, it will be difficult to control your golf swing. The exercises below are designed to refine your awareness of physical tensions and emotion, since they have a direct bearing on the smoothness and rhythm of your golf swing.

Body Scanning

- Several times a day stop doing whatever you are doing and pay attention to the amount of tension/relaxation and warmth/coolness that exist in various parts of your body—head, neck, shoulders, arms, wrists, hands, fingers, chest, abdomen, back, hips, thighs, knees, calves, ankles, feet, toes.

Physical Sensations Related to Swinging a Golf Club

- Increase and decrease the amount of tension in your hands, wrists, and forearms separately as you make a number of shots; the tension should vary from very loose to very tight. Notice the quality of the shots as you vary the tension.
- Immediately after making a fine shot reproduce the swing and become aware of the amount of tension you feel in your legs, shoulders, hands, wrists, and forearms. Do the same thing after making a poor shot. Determine the differences in muscle tension between the good and bad shot.
- With your eyes closed or blindfolded, have someone hand you a club selected randomly. Swing the club and identify which one it is. Repeat with other clubs. Do this until you can identify any club without looking at it. Becoming keenly aware of the differences in the heft of each of your clubs will make it easier for you to adjust your basic swing from shot to shot.

Emotional Awareness

You probably know that emotions affect muscle tension, and therefore are closely linked to your golf swing. Emotional states can either facilitate or disrupt your game. Anger at yourself after making a poor shot, for example, usually increases muscle tension in your hands and wrists, causing you to grab the club in a death grip. Muscle tension can also affect swing tempo. In both cases the quality of a shot is affected. The following exercises will help you to increase your emotional awareness.

- Each time you become aware of a strong emotion on the golf course, scan your body to identify the specific physical sensations that accompany it. For example, clenched fists suggest anger, butterflies in the stomach usually means fear, and tightness in the leg muscles could mean frustration. Notice the most intense sensations related to each emotional state and how that tension affects the quality of your golf shots.
- Experiment with increasing and then decreasing tension in the muscles associated with a particular emotion identified in the previous exercise. Is there any change in your emotional state? Again notice how it affects your golf shots.
- When an emotion—for instance, anger, frustration, worry, or fear—becomes too strong on the course, decrease tension in the muscles associated with the emotion, look upward and make an internal image of a pleasant scene. Is there is a reduction in emotional intensity? Do your shots improve?

APPENDIX C

Guide to Selecting Metaskills Techniques

This appendix is a ready reference and guide to selecting appropriate metaskills techniques to achieve various outcomes. It contains two parts: (1) an alphabetical listing of the techniques and the purposes they serve; and (2) an alphabetical listing of common outcomes and the techniques that can be used to achieve them.

To secure detailed information about each technique refer to the page references in parentheses. The index may also be used to locate anecdotes related to the various techniques.

Techniques and the Purposes They Serve

Anchoring (pp. 29, 41)

Improve memory.
Stabilize a state of consciousness.

Change a state of consciousness quickly.
Apply inner resources.
Improve concentration.
Increase confidence.
Increase energy.
Facilitate unconscious control of performance.
Increase consistency of performance.
Stabilize swing effort

Backup Process (pp. 165, 166)

Identify outcomes.
Prepare for tournaments.
Analyze setup and swing.

Body Scanning (p. 188)

Increase awareness of emotional states.
Increase awareness of swing effort.
Increase ability to analyze swing mechanics.
Facilitate use of Uptime Anchor.
Facilitate use of Discovering Difference.

Colored-Image Anchor (p. 81)

Maintain consistency of performance.
Stabilize emotional state.

Competitive-State Anchor (pp. 62, 63)

Control anxiety during competition.
Maintain an optimum competitive state.
Prepare for a forthcoming tournament.

Counting Process (p. 79)

Regulate swing tempo.

Cross-over Training (p. 182)

Improve capacity to make internal images.
Increase sensitivity to bodily sensations.
Increase sensitivity to swing effort.
Increase sensitivity to sound.
Improve capacity to become aware of internal dialogue.
Improve capacity to read greens.
Improve club selection.

Discovering Difference (pp. 90, 93)

Reduce confusion.
Increase consistency of performance.
Identify significant setup and swing keys.

Effort Control (p. 104, 121)

Identify and control the amount of swing effort.
Improve club selection.
Determine the line and speed of putts.

Energy Anchor (p. 142)

Maintain an energized state.
Overcome fatigue.

Energy Visualization (p. 142)

Establish and maintain an energized state.
Speed up recovery from fatigue.

Establishing Outcomes (pp. 162, 169)

Identify worthwhile outcomes.
Specify precisely what you want to accomplish.
Develop positive outlook.
Maintain focused practice sessions.

Free-Swing Anchor (p. 82)

Control swing effort.
Regulate swing tempo.
Stabilize emotional state.
Increase consistency of performance.

Get-It Process (pp. 94, 99)

Learn new shots.
Improve shots.
Determine swing effort.

Get-It-Back Process (p. 96)

Relearn shots.
Determine swing effort.

Golf-Shot Resource Anchor (pp. 56, 60)

Increase consistency of performance.
Increase confidence.
Facilitate unconscious control of performance.

Greenprinting (p. 111)

Improve ability to read greens.

Holographic Viewing (p. 101)

Analyze performance.
Acquire new skills.
Improve existing skills.

Inside Out (pp. 145, 147)

Reduce or eliminate pain.

Mechanical Just-Right Anchor (pp. 53, 54)

Increase consistency of performance.
Increase concentration.

M & M Process (pp. 72, 74)

Change emotional state quickly.
Stabilize emotional state.
Establish and maintain swing tempo.
Regulate swing effort.
Establish and maintain playing pace.
Increase consistency of performance.

Metaphors (p. 100)

Improve concentration.
Maintain swing consistency.
Create optimal performance state.
Regulate energy level.

Metaskills Healing (p. 153)

Speed up healing.
Heal without surgery or medication.

Meta Pictures (p. 184)

Analyze setup and swing.
Reduce intensity of uncomfortable feelings.
Gain a new perspective.

Multiple Images (p. 185)

Improve consistency of swing path.
Read greens.

Off-Ramp Technique (p. 79)

Regulate swing tempo.

Paradoxical Intention (p. 102)

Increase swing control.
Increase consistency of performance.
Increase confidence.

Personal Power Anchor (pp. 64, 67)

Overcome anxiety.
Tap resources of excellence and effectiveness.
Build confidence.

Piece-of-Cake Anchor (pp. 75, 77)

Make tough shots easy.
Increase confidence.
Increase consistency of performance.

Self-hypnosis (Betty Erickson Technique) (pp. 123, 128, 138)

Maintain concentration.
Develop relaxed state.
Access long-forgotten experiences.
Control pain.
Create a just-right state.
Distort perception of time.
Access mental strategies.
Identify central setup and swing keys.
Facilitate healing.
Build trust in the unconscious mind.
Change unwanted habit patterns.
Improve performance.
Analyze performance.
Build confidence.

Sherlock Holmes Exercise (pp. 16, 23)

Understand how you process information.
Analyze how you mentally regulate playing the game.
Identify elements of strategies.
Improve memory.
Identify internal resources from past experiences.

Recall past golf shots.
Identify important setup and swing keys.
Identify just-right states.
Facilitate getting into an altered state.

"Shouldniks" (p. 160)

Reduce compulsive behavior.
Identify worthwhile outcomes.

"Swish" (pp. 83, 86, 148)

Change emotional state.
Reduce or eliminate pain.

Uptime Anchor (pp. 48, 52)

Identify important setup and swing keys.
Increase concentration.
Increase consistency of performance.

Video Observation (pp. 137, 138)

Analyze swing.
Increase consistency.
Learn new shots.

V-K Weave (pp. 116, 117)

Identify swing effort.
Increase control of clubhead speed.
Improve club selection.

Outcomes and the Techniques to Use

Below is a list of typical outcomes and the metaskills techniques that can be used to achieve them.

Anxiety Control

Competitive-State Anchor
Mechanical Just-Right Anchor
Personal Power Anchor
Self-hypnosis
"Swish"

Chipping

Effort Control
Greenprinting
V-K Weave

Club Selection

Effort Control
V-K Weave

Concentration

Discovering Difference
M & M Process
Metaphors
Self-hypnosis
Uptime Anchor

Confidence

Competitive-State Anchor
Golf-Shot Resource Anchor
Paradoxical Intention
Personal Power Anchor
Self-hypnosis

Confusion, Reducing

Discovering Difference
Effort Control

Establishing Outcomes
Uptime Anchor

Consistency of Performance

Colored-Image Anchor
Competitive-State Anchor
Discovering Difference
Effort Control
Mechanical Just-Right Anchor
Piece-of-Cake Anchor
Uptime Anchor
Video Observation
V-K Weave

Fatigue, Reducing

Energy Anchor
Energy Visualization

Healing

Metaskills Healing
Self-hypnosis

Improving Shots

Backup Process
Effort Control
Get-It-Back Process
Greenprinting
Holographic Viewing
Mechanical Just-Right Anchor
Sherlock Holmes Exercise
Video Observation
V-K Weave

Learning New Shots

Get-It Process
Holographic Viewing
Video Observation

Outcomes, Determining

Backup Process
Establishing Outcomes

Pain Control

Inside Out
Self-hypnosis
"Swish"

Putting

Discovering Difference
Effort Control
Get-It and Get-It-Back Process
Greenprinting
Mechanical Just-Right Anchor
Video Observation
V-K Weave

Setup Analysis

Backup Process
Discovering Difference
Holographic Viewing
Self-hypnosis
Sherlock Holmes Exercise
Uptime Anchor

Short Game

Cross-over Training
Effort Control

Greenprinting
V-K Weave

Stabilize State

Anchoring
M & M Process
Metaphors
"Swish"

State Change

Energy Anchor
Mechanical Just-Right Anchor
M & M Process
Meta Pictures
Self-hypnosis
"Swish"

Swing Analysis

Backup Process
Discovering Difference
Effort Control
Holographic Viewing
Meta Pictures
Self-hypnosis
Sherlock Holmes Exercise
Uptime Anchor
Video Observation

Swing Effort

Colored-Image Anchor
Effort Control
Free-Swing Anchor
Get-It Process
Greenprinting

M & M Process
Video Observation
V-K Weave

Swing Tempo

Counting Process
Effort Control
Free-Swing Anchor
M & M Process
Metaphors
Off-Ramp Technique
Video Observation

Tournament Preparation

Backup Process
Competitive-State Anchor
Effort Control
Self-hypnosis
Video Observation

The "Yips"

Effort Control
Greenprinting
Sherlock Holmes Exercise

INDEX